Marrakech

Footprint

Justin McGuinness

Contents

About the author

Justin McGuinness has travelled widely in North Africa since 1980, when he was an undergraduate studying Arabic at Cambridge. He lived in Tunis for many years, before returning to England to take a PhD in urban planning. In Marrakech, he lived for spells in Derb Debbachi, Guéliz and even got as far as Massira II. At present he lives in Paris.

Acknowledgements

Credit is due to numerous friends and acquaintances for all their help and advice. Bernard Rubio came up with many a nugget of insider information, Zoubeïr Mouhli explained the mysteries of médina and medersa, Abderrahime Kassou provided insight on rural architecture, and Jacqueline Alluchon got the writer hooked on Moroccan carpets. Jim Miller and David Bond helped with some judicious proof-reading. Credit is due to all those in and around Marrakech who shared thoughts and ideas about their city. Thanks as well go to AR Ben Chemsi and Ahmed Yahia for the discussions on contemporary Morocco. And thanks, as always, to Mum and Dad for all their support.

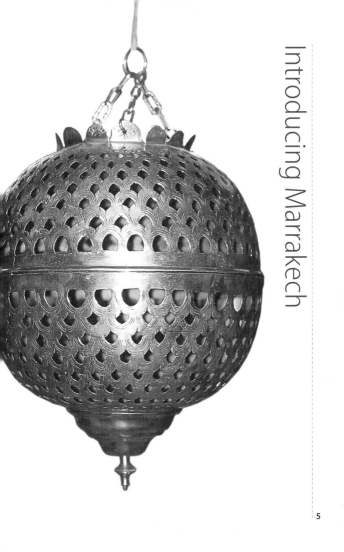

Marrakech: the word strikes the ear like a hot desert wind thrashing through the palm groves. Surrounded by adobe ramparts, set in an oasis, a short flight from Europe, by rights this Red City should only exist in a fevered sultana's dreams and, in a sense, Marrakech is a city built on pure imagination. Historic glories may be a little thin on the ground – the fortifications are old rather than ancient, great monuments are somewhat scarce, new neighbourhoods sprawl ever outwards, eating into the palm groves, and the main avenue is now clogged with traffic – but still the tourists come, lured by the colour, the light, the promise of some longed-for sensuality. No fading flower of a city, Marrakech *is* colour – as any ramble in the souks shows. Perhaps the city's earth-red walls and green palms inspired the Moroccan flag: a green Solomon's seal on scarlet ground. Could it be that local temperament owes something to this colour contrast, too? Flashes of enthusiasm mesh with happy-go-lucky warmth. And above all the Marrakchis are *bahja* – joyful, vivid, living for the good times. No wonder their city is known as Morocco's pleasure capital.

6

Drink and look

Deep in the old town, a famous fountain is known to all as *chrob wa chouf*, 'drink and look'. Rendez-vous here. The fountain's geometric jigsaw surface of tiny tiles is like the city: kaleidoscopic. On a summer's day, a wander in the médina-maze does more than parch you: it massages all the senses. You'll gulp down Sidi Ali water, you'll gaze on all the postcard clichés – and pick up on a hundred minor pleasures. Lose yourself in labyrinths of light and shade, then take a horse-drawn *calèche*, the gondola of Marrakech, through moped fumes to 'la Place', Jemaâ el Fna, the city's hippy-collage of a centre and pulsating home to unforeseen encounters, storytellers, mythomaniacs.

Sheherazade's place

And if the city were personified, who would it be? Paunchy bazaar merchant, hospitable but venal? The médina girl adopting urchin airs to wheedle a tourist dirham? Veiled Nada, patron of the internet café? Or an ever-marginal itinerant storyteller? Beneath its coloured surface, there is more to jovial, jostling Marrakech than meets the eye. The city is as unfathomable as the snow-capped High Atlas mountains, visible from médina rooftops on a spring day.

Into the High Atlas

The Red City is the daughter of the Atlas. Mountain melt-water sustains the oasis town down on the arid Haouz. And after the heaving fleshpots of Marrakech, a mountain fastness will be a welcome relief. The High Atlas is a land of shattered rock plateaux and green valleys, deep gorges and shale drops. Here adobe villages and miniature terraced fields reveal a people who long survived in harmony with their harsh environment. The 21st-century ideology of tourist individualism – on a potentially massive scale – remains in the city of the plain. Quest for the essence of exotica in Marrakech if you like, but its time spent in the sunburned uplands of the Atlas really gives life a new strangeness.

At a glance

Jemaâ el Fna

Visitors to Marrakech inevitably converge on the médina, a labyrinth of narrow streets and alleyways. The epicentre, Jemaâ el Fna or 'la Place' is a uniquely irregular urban space for varied and bizarre entertainments. Here beats the médina's heart, pulsating late into the night with singers and snake-charmers, knaves and drummers, tinkerly acrobats and tattoo artists. Now designated a World Heritage Site, witness to the ancient arts of storytelling, Jemaâ el Fna has survived the developers' designs to become the city's symbol – along with the nearby minaret of the Koutoubia Mosque. Kids will be entranced by the pick-n-mix universe of characters at loose across the square.

North of Jemaâ el Fna

Once a caravan city, Marrakech still has great commercial prowess, as the mass conversion of old riads into profitable exotic holiday retreats reveals. Today, the covered market streets north of Jemaâ el Fna are devoted to satisfying visitors' desires for leather slippers and dates, wrought iron mirror frames and brass bibelots. Foreign arty types have also brought a welcome contemporary twist to the craft tradition. Where the souks run out, more sights await the culturally minded: the Musée de Marrakech and the largest Islamic college in Morocco, the Medersa Ben Youssef, high-point of the city's decorative arts. Nearby is Marrakech's oldest building, the blocky Almoravid Koubba. A wander in this part of the city naturally leads eastward to the pungent tanneries, where leather is still made to ancestral recipes. Also in the maze of dusty alleys north of the square are palaces for the best Moroccan nosh.

South of Jemaâ el Fna: the Palace quarter

Real tourists make an early start to do the area south of Jemaâ el Fna. Here are the serious sites: craft collections in patio palaces, the tombs of the 16th-century Saâdians – the most bijou royal mausoleum in Islam? You might even locate a semi-abandoned synagogue, witness to a time before base homeland politics destroyed religious co-existence. A long hike will take you down to the Agdal gardens through neighbourhoods of pink-washed walls and hole-in-the-wall shops. From rambling nests atop ramparts, storks flap off to pick through the city rubbish dumps, a horse-drawn calèche squeezes down a side-street.

Guéliz and the Hivernage

There are no real must-see sites in Guéliz, once Marrakech's *ville nouvelle*, reached from the médina by the first tree-planted boulevard outside the city walls, Avenue Mohammed V. Guéliz is a place where until recently low-key luxury met provincial Morocco. However, new concrete blocks, tourist coaches and a McDonald's have knocked the edge off the 1930s elegance. Still, ladies who lunch promenade their pooches on quiet streets under the orange trees, (fairly) respectable gents sup a beer at the Café Atlas, and local youths on vespas screech up to the Colisée to take in a film. For the visitor, Guéliz is where you find restaurants with airs and graces, pizzas and pasta joints, and bars seedier than a rotting watermelon.

South of Guéliz, the Hivernage is a showcase of colonial planning, a garden city for winter residence. On curving suburban streets, hidden in greenery, hotels sit next to modernist villas. In the shade of a well-groomed hedge, machine-gun toting soldiers indicate a royal in residence. Cutting across the Hivernage, the link between Guéliz and the projected Oliveraie hotel zone, the Avenue de France will be Marrakech's Champs Elysées. Here sits the squat red mass of the Palais des Congrès, home to many an international incentive seminar. Jauntier and closer to Guéliz is the Théâtre Royal, all domes and Pharaonic detailing. Could it bring that longed-for gust of cultural energy? For the moment, the annual artsy ciné fest at the Colisée and the outdoor theatre of the Institut français are focal points of Marrakech's artistic life.

The Palmeraie

North and east of the city is hedonists' Marrakech, the Palmeraie. In the 1970s, this was still – just about – the city's lung, a place where market gardens glowed green under the dusty date palms. Drought and the decay of traditional irrigation blighted the area – until bright sparks realized that this was prime development land. Today, high walls and building sites among the palms show that ready cash is being ploughed into conspicuous consumption such as that seen in both European and Moroccan deco-mags. Never have the city's craft builders been busier.

The High Atlas

Antidote to Red City summers are the cool valleys of the Atlas mountains, a 90-minute drive away. Though often swathed in heat-haze, the ever snow-capped backdrop of the tourist brochures merits a side-trip. With four-wheel drive vehicles visitors can reach isolated adobe villages once accessible only to mules and walkers. In a remote valley, the roofless grandeur of the mosque of Tin Mal testifies to a vanished dynasty's power. In the Ouarzazate direction – and still within day-trip distance – is another striking high pass, the Tizi-n-Tichka, and the village of Telouet where a pacha's palace, all Berber-baronial splendour, crumbles back into earth.

The Atlantic coast

Marrakech has ocean boltholes as well as mountain hideaways. One-time hippy destination, rediscovered by Paris intellectuals in the 1980s, Essaouira became a happening spot in the late 1990s and now has an airport to prove it. Here the surf-bums play footie with the locals and ecological retreats are opening in the countryside. Further north, phosphate port Safi, famed for craft pottery, is far too rough for gentrifiers and oyster town Oualidia, somnolent outside summer, struggles to maintain a reputation as Marrakech's St Tropez. Thankfully, things have not reached such a pass.

Trip planner

Sunny days are plentiful in Marrakech. The climate is dry all year round, with thunderstorms in early autumn and occasional downpours in winter. The best times to visit are late spring and early autumn, when the days are still long enough to get plenty of sightseeing in. Winter is pleasant with bright days – and you could even nip up to Oukaïmeden in the Atlas to see the snow. In summer, the temperatures can rise to 40°C and although the days are long, the heat haze masks mountain views. Essaouira has a more temperate climate than Marrakech, rarely rising above 26°C and never less than 10°C. From March to mid-September, the alizé winds blow, to the delight of windsurfers but others can find the constant wind trying. (Winter is a better time for other surfers.) If you want to do some hiking, May and June are a good months. The snows have gone from all but the highest peaks and the heat has yet to come down.

The summer low season in Marrakech is a thing of the past – although riad prices tend to be lower. Christmas and New Year are very busy, and May sees large numbers of French visitors taking extra days off work to bridge between bank holidays. Summer is busy with French-born Moroccans back spending time with family. The month of **Ramadan** is not the ideal time to visit Marrakech. (In 2004, Ramadan begins on 15 October and ends 12 November. The start of the month moves forward 11 days each year.) During this time, Moroccans refrain from eating and drinking during daylight hours, which means that tempers fray and service and driving standards deteriorate somewhat. Life is a bit painful for smokers and those who like a drink, as many bars close too.

Two months after the end of Ramadan comes **Aïd el Kebir**, 'the feast of the sacrifice' and the major holiday of the Muslim calendar. The next Aïd will be 31 January 2005. Public transport gets very busy, as this is a time when people take a week's break to get back to their *bled* (home towns).

★ Ten of the best

1 **Breakfast** *Bghir* crèpes and honey in a riad garden, p102.

2 **Jemaâ el Fna** Aka 'la Place', p37. The great open area where main Av Mohammed V meets the old town. At its liveliest in late afternoon – when the light is better for photographs from (say) terrace of Café CTM. Sundown snapshots of the Koutoubia through barbecue fumes. Will you go for pâtisserie at the Argana or steamed snails, p132?

3 **Palace Quarter** Spend a morning visiting the big historic sites south of Jemaâ el Fna: don't miss the ruined Badi Palace. Down a canyon-like passageway lies a vast walled enclosure, tranquil after the heaving streets. In a far chamber is the medieval *minbar* of the Koutoubia Mosque, p52.

4 **Pâtisserie des Princes** Burn your fingers and get grease on your jeans wolfing down a mini-pastilla, p133.

5 **Avenue Mohammed V** Enjoy the spring smells: horse manure and orange blossom. Buy individual cigarettes from street vendors and in the evening take a look at the fun fair and the motorcyclist at the 'wall of death', p59.

6 **Medinate** Head for the architectural sights and end up 'medinating' in the old town: does argan oil *really* cure acne?

7 **Hammam du Pacha** Stretch and sweat on the heated marble floor of a Moorish bath, perhaps the decaying but still splendid Hammam in Dar el Bacha, p193.

8 **Post-prandial boogie** In a médina restaurant, undulate hands and hips with a real *danseuse orientale*, p129.

9 **Make a wish** At Jardin Majorelle's fishpond p60.

10 **Safi** The gritty phosphate port. Drive across the Plateau des Gantours to this most un-bijou of Morocco's historic Atlantic ports. Visit the potters' quarter, see the catch being brought in, explore the decaying médina, p93.

24 hours

With a day free at the end of a conference or hiking trip, you can just about cram in the main sights of Marrakech and still have a large Moroccan evening meal. Starting early, get to the sights in the 'Museum Quarter' south of **Jemaâ el Fna**. Visit the **Saâdian tombs** and the **great palaces** (the ruined Badi', the Dar Si Saïd for its museum). Textile and carpet buffs must not miss the **Maison Tiskiouine**. After a very small lunch (in Guéliz or a cheap place off Jemaâ el Fna) return to your hotel for a siesta before tackling the northern part of the médina. Find your way through from chic **Mouassine** via the **Medersa Ben Youssef** to **Bab Debbagh**, home of that smelliest of attractions, the **tanneries**. Expect to get slightly lost before someone guides you to the main souks for shopping. As the sun goes down, get back to Jemaâ el Fna to see the entertainments. Unless you've reserved for slap-up Marrakchi gastronomics at a discreet **riad restaurant** in the médina, eat at one of the barbecue restaurants on 'la Place'. Try a bowl of steamed snails, for example.

Two-four days

Two days allows you to cover the big sights of Marrakech and take a trip up into the Atlas, possibly with a tour company although a hire car gives you most freedom. If time is limited, a trip to **Imlil** takes you closest to mountain village life. (NB Last section of road deteriorates to track). A **Ouirgane/Tin Mal** excursion should take priority over a trip to the Glaoui palace at **Telouet**. Two Atlantic port towns, **Essaouira** (beautiful but increasingly tripperish) and **Safi** (historic ramparts, potteries, rougher atmosphere) can be done as a day trips from Marrakech. Prefer share-taxis over buses to get there and back, although there is a good Supratours bus service to Essaouira. Note that the last share taxi back to Marrakech generally leaves in the late afternoon. Obviously, an overnight in Essaouira gives you a better sense of place.

One week or more

A week is enough to cover Marrakech and region thoroughly. For those with an interest in things architectural (and a hire car), three days is enough to cover Marrakech thoroughly whilst taking it at a relatively easy pace. A long half day to do the Palace quarter and another long half day for the souks, the Musée de Marrakech and the Medersa Ben Youssef. The head for **Essaouira** for a relaxing couple of days on the Ocean. From Essaouira, **Safi** is an easy day trip, too. In spring or early autumn, contrast the bustle of Marrakech with a couple of sleepy days at the small resort of **Oualidia**, eating at the fish restaurants. Another option is to loop across the spectacular **Tizi-n-Test** pass to Taroudant, Marrakech's 'little sister', for a night, then up to Essaouira. The Tizi-n-Test route is for drivers with a good head for heights. In a week, you could also contrast Marrakech with three nights up in the mountains, doing a spot of walking out of **Setti Fatma** or **Imlil/Aremd**. Riding can be arranged at Ouirgane.

Two weeks

With two weeks, you could go for the relaxing option (a week based in Marrakech, exploring the city, doing some side trips, followed by a week in Essaouira). However, a week in Essaouira might be a bit long, unless you are into surf-sports or watercolour painting. Combine Marrakech and Essaouira in week one followed by a trip over the Atlas to Ouarzazate and the Dadès Valley on the second week, preferably by hire car. For keen walkers, two weeks will give you excellent hiking in the High Atlas of Toubkal (or the High Atlas of Azilal, see Footprint Morocco Handbook), followed by a day tacked on the end to whizz round Marrakech.

Contemporary Marrakech

Marrakech, *Mareksh* in spoken Arabic, is a city which gave its name to a kingdom. In 17th-century engravings, it is labelled 'Morocco City'. In the Amazigh pun, the city is *ma-ra-kish*, 'the place where they'll eat you if they can'. Marrakech is southern Morocco's metropolis, a lodestone for the rural poor. Displayed in international deco-magazines, its profile as pleasure city, source of ethno-Moorish chic, has never been higher and the growing number of foreign residents refer to the city as RAK – for its airport code.

Marrakech starts in history as an imperial capital. When William the Conqueror was occupying England, the future RAK was terminus for trans-Saharan caravans. In 1070, veiled warriors led by one Youssef ibn Tachfine swept up from the Sahara. Supplies of gold and slaves from West Africa were under their control. A major camp was created north of the Atlas Mountains – where thousands of palm trees sprouted, since military lunchpacks were filled with dates. By the time of ibn Tachfine's death in 1106, the campsite was a walled city, capital of an empire stretching from Senegal to Madrid, from the Atlantic to Kabylia. A century later, another warrior dynasty, the purist Almohads, gave the city its greatest monument, the minaret of the Koutoubia Mosque, now to Marrakech what Big Ben is to London. But this is not a city of sanctified built heritage, no Venice of the Orient. Marrakech never worshipped stones, its monuments are evanescent – to the disappointment of tour-operators. In the theatre-square of Jemaâ el Fna, alongside acrobats and snakecharmers, the storytellers still tell their tales. And by their very nature, stories leave traces only in the mind.

Of course, the finest point to scan the Red City would be the summit of the Koutoubia. But Moroccan minarets are off-limits to all but *muezzins*. Happily a more secular vantage point exists, an anti-Koutoubia: the roof-top bar of the *Café La Renaissance*, six storeys above and 2 km down the main thoroughfare in Guéliz, RAK's 'European' other half.

Panoptic viewpoints aside, the core of Marrakech has two distinct quarters. The division, dating from colonial times, corresponded to two very different mentalities. The walled médina is *bildi*, traditional. In 1912, when the French took over, the médina was the city, home to a decadent court and an illiterate populace, artisans whose tools had barely changed in a hundred years or so, *imams* whose learning went back much further. Children headed to the storytellers on the square for entertainment. In the 1920s, smooth modernist Guéliz was built west of the médina. Here things are *roumi*, clean and convenient. There are villas, cafés and bars, streets for cars, a cinema. While educated homes may have books on soufism and Islamic calligraphy, the kids will be in the French school. Mother shops in Casablanca, father runs a factory: a firm has relocated from Europe.

Beyond Guéliz and Douar Laskar – the military quarter – the new Marrakech stretches out into the Haouz Plain. Geographically and architecturally *roumi*, Massiras I, II and III are *bildi* by mindset. They don't speak much French in the stilt-legged blocks of Massiras I and II, while Massira III hides villas behind high walls, protected by resident gardiens, it also has the city's best hammam. South of the médina lies SYBA, acronym for Sidi Youssef ben Ali. Named for one of the city's seven saints, the former bidonville now has tarmac streets and a garden promenade where courting couples – he in jeans, she with trendy headscarf – enjoy the evening air.

But neighbourhood distinctions are blurring. Speeding, squealing mopeds get everywhere, undulating Arabic glows neon on shopfronts across the city. In the médina, 40-something advertising executives, overwhelmed by their Parisian *ennui de vivre*, are buying up the garden palaces. Proximity to drinking holes no longer stops Marrakchi families from enjoying bourgeois respectability in Guéliz. Old town alleys find room for cyber cafés, the best caftan shops are in the ville nouvelle. And halfway down Avenue Mohammed V, the global smell of McDonalds' frying fat fills the air. Further down, the dusty, owl-haunted orange grove by the Koutoubia has given way to a municipal rose garden to put an English seaside town to shame. Wrought iron curlicues imprison the city's most venerable sight and ancestor of Gothic: the Almoravid dome.

Médina notes. Smells of cedar dust and horse dung, coriander, varnish and dust. Dawn: cocks crowing from the terraces, call to prayer. Night: cats fighting in an alley, orange glow of ochre walls in street light. Every morning, on the shady side of the street, *moul likama*, the mint seller, lays out his vivid green leafy bundles on plastic sacking. Behind him, the girl on the jawwal poster is toothily cheerful: Maroc-Télécom provides text-messaging for all.

The growing mix of the *roumi* and the *bildi* doesn't seem to disturb local pride in the Red City. There is not much notion of unbroken descent here: this was always a crossroads town. Caravan port, capital of colonial control, refuge for the rural poor, Marrakech has added 'orientalist playground for the über-rich' to its CV. Here all manner of freewheelers find opportunity: an ageing gigolo turns up-scale restaurateur, a wideboy reworks tales from the Arabian Nights in mesmerizing Ali-Baba shows, complete with flying carpets and cavalry charges, all in a purpose-built desert complex. The Menara olive groves have son et lumière. In the first years of Mohammed VI's reign (1999-present), the climate is on the optimistic side, international events notwithstanding. The price of bread (and other basics), key to the temper of the whole city, has remained stable. The incoming *nasranis*, as the Europeans are called, are observed and, on the whole, appreciated.

And on a bright winter morning, somewhere in the médina, stuck between a mobylette belching smoke and a large lady draped in a synthetic turquoise *djellaba*, you may be tempted, too. A shady voice in your ear says, 'Want to see a riad for sale?' Is this an offer too good to miss? A few minutes and a blind alley later you're under the medlar trees in a tiled courtyard. The owner, a woman in her 60s, finds herself alone in a rambling home. The children are in Rabat, reliable servants to sloosh down stairs and

Entrance to the Koutoubia Mosque
Marrakech's most famous landmark. As the Eiffel Tower is to Paris, so its minaret (see also p1) is to the Red City.

clean cool, high ceilinged rooms are so hard to find … How much? *Pas cherrrr.* How much? *Combien vous pouvez donner?* From the terrace, a chaos of wires and chicken sheds, pergolas and distant minarets, mountains somewhere in the haze. A stork flaps lazily by, a palm tree cranes over a neighbouring wall. The melancholy of an old family house could so easily be transformed. Introspective and exuberant by turns, Marrakech has won another convert.

But this new convert can spend in a single day what a whole family lives on for a month – as can a middle class Moroccan, for that matter. How has revolution been avoided? Remember: the Marrakchis are good-timers and, some will say, they've seen many an invasion before. Far from xenophobic, they've become past masters in satisfying the whims of the médina's new denizens. Favours are exchanged, a network of personal ties develops as old properties rise from crumbling ruin to tasteful *résidence secondaire*. For the moment, there is no sign of tumbrils rolling onto Jemaâ el Fna. Light gantries on 'la Place' for *raï* concerts attracting thousands are the nearest that 'la Place' has got to a scaffold – so far.

And then the incomers of all sorts, both Moroccan and foreign, slip unprotesting into to the Red City's rhythm. On a long, hot médina ramble, your pace inevitably slackens. Does it really matter that you don't get to the carpet shop for four fifteen? Dump the minutes on your digital *magana*, the riddles in the souk need answers, an old acquaintance has turned up, the incident was unforeseen. How could things be otherwise in a city where people ride three up on a moped with a sheep, where trance-dance meets tourist pack on a daily basis? Red City time is somehow malleable, elastic. It takes a working day for the local culinary treat, *tanjia* – lamb baked slowly in the embers of the hammam oven (see p134) – to cook, at least an hour for the chants of the city's most emblematic music form, the drum-beat *dakka*, to reach a climax. The only oasis city north of the Atlas Mountains, Marrakech retains the slowness of the desert in its soul.

From London and Paris, there are direct scheduled flights to Marrakech. There are also frequent scheduled and charter flights from Europe, Canada, the Middle East and West Africa to Casablanca with connecting flights to Marrakech. Otherwise take the train (nearly 3 hours) or CTM bus.

It is also possible to travel to Morocco from France (Sète) and Spain (Algeciras, Almería) by ferry. Most travellers find the Algeciras to Tangiers (or Ceuta) crossing most practical. There is a rail link from Tangiers to Marrakech via Casablanca.

Marrakech is a compact, flat city. From the heart of the médina (old town) to Guéliz it is a 40-minute walk or 10 minutes in a petit taxi. There are regular bus services on this route. If you are staying in the Palmeraie, a taxi or a bicycle will be necessary to get to the médina.

Destinations in the High Altas region south of Marrakech are best reached by share-taxi (usually a big Mercedes). There is a good bus service to Essaouira. All the Atlantic coast destinations covered here (Essaouira, Safi and Oualidia) can be reached by share-taxi.

Getting there

Air

From the UK and the rest of Europe Direct flights to Marrakech are operated by **Royal Air Maroc** (RAM), **Air France** and **British Airways**. Prices are highest over the end of year break and will be heavily booked during the two main Muslim holidays Aïd es Seghir (end of Ramadan) and two months after that for Aïd el Kebir. The direct scheduled flights from London cost anything from around £250-400). In winter flights are usually scheduled so that it is possible to leave London on a Thursday evening or Friday lunchtime and return on a Sunday or Tuesday afternoon.

Charter flights or package holidays can work out cheaper than buying just a flight. Some UK-based charter companies buy space on scheduled flights. In particular, try **Safar Travel**, 94-96 Seymour Road, London W1H 1ND, **T** 020-7724-2211; and **Inspirations**, Victoria House, Victoria Road, Horley, Surrey, RH6 7AD, **T** 01293-822244. See also the websites listed on the next page for more good deals.

French charter company **Mondair** runs direct flights from Paris – Charles de Gaulle and French provincial cities to Marrakech. Flights range from €300-500, depending on conditions and time of year. Flying time from Paris to Marrakech is around 3 hours 20 minutes.

The London or Paris to Marrakech services excepted, the vast majority of the RAM and other airline services from Europe to Morocco touch down in the country's economic capital, Casablanca (Aéroport Mohammed V). There are flights from Amsterdam, Bordeaux, Brussels, Copenhagen, Düsseldorf, Frankfurt, Geneva, Madrid, Málaga, Marseille, Milan, Munich, Nice, Paris, Rome, Stockholm, Strasbourg, Toulouse, Vienna and Zürich. If you take a direct flight to Casablanca, followed by a RAM connecting internal flight, note that you may have a longish wait in Casablanca airport. (Two hours is not enough time to get into Casablanca, see the sights and get back through airport security,

→ Airlines and agents

Airlines

Alitalia, **T** 0874-5448259, www.alitalia.it
Air France, **T** 0845-0845111, www.airfrance.com
British Airways **T** 0845-7733377, www.britishairways.com
Iberia, **T** 0845-6012854, www.iberia.es
KLM, **T** 0870-5074047, www.klm.com
Lufthansa, **T** 0845-7737747, www.lufthansa.com
Qantas, **T** 0845-7747767, www.qantas.com
Royal Air Maroc, **T** 020-74398854, 020-74394361,
www.royalairmaroc.com
Singapore Airlines, **T** 213-1011, www.singaporeair.com
Virgin Atlantic, **T** 1800-8628621, www.virgin-atlantic.com

Agents

www.cheapflights.com
www.expedia.com
www.flynow.com
www.istc.org
www.safartravel.co.uk
www.statravel.com
www.travelocity.com

tightened up considerably since the bomb-attacks of May 2003.) With a connection at Casablanca, total flying and waiting time can be anything from 6-9 hours. On a long break, it is best to touch down in Casablanca and take the train to Marrakech.

From Canada and the USA As there are a large number of Moroccan emigrants in Québec, **Royal Air Maroc** (RAM) runs flights to Casablanca from Montréal and, for the moment, New York. (Flight time New York to Casablanca, 6 hours 40 mins.) Alternatively, travel to Europe with **British Airways**, **Air France**, or **KLM** all of which have flights to Moroccan destinations. The **Tunisair** flight between Tunis and Montréal also touches down in Casablanca.

From Australia and New Zealand There are no direct flights to Morocco from either country. Your best bet is a flight to Paris or London with **Qantas** from where you can pick up a connection.

Airport information **Aéroport Marrakech Menara**, **T** 044-447862, Marrakech's airport is 6 km outside the city and a 20-minute taxi ride from the médina or 15 minutes from Guéliz. The airport has been expanded since the late 1990s to cater for the growing number of passengers. In the arrivals hall after customs, there are several cash dispensers. Banks **BMCE** and **Banque Populaire** have *bureaux de change* which stay open until the last flight's arrivals have gone through. Car hire stands are also in the arrivals hall. Taxis are the only really viable option for getting to town from the airport, as the number 11 bus stops too far (nearly 1 km) from the airport. A grand taxi should not set you back more than 50dh (60dh at night), for the run from airport to Guéliz, the modern town. Taxi drivers may accept foreign currency.

Aéroport Casablanca Mohammed V, Casablanca's main airport, at Nouasseur, 30 km southeast of Casablanca, **T** 022-339100, has all the features of a big international airport – bar hotels. As you come onto the main concourse after customs, there are cash dispensers and bureaux de change just ahead of you. Onward travel to the centre is by shuttle train or taxi. (The train station Casa-Port is under the main airport concourse.) For train travel to Marrakech, you must go to Casa-Voyageurs station. See below for further details. The **CTM** bus station (www.ctm.co.ma for timetables) for buses to Marrakech is behind the Tour Habous, on Av des FAR. Car hire companies, including Sixt, Budget, and Herz as well as local companies, are on the main concourse to your left as you come out through the frosted glass doors.

→ Travel extras

Entry No visas are required for full passport holders of EU countries, Australia, Canada, New Zealand/Aotearoa and the USA. Your passport should have at least 6 months' validity remaining. On arrival, you will be required to fill in a form with standard passport details. EU visitors are given entry for three months.

Money The monetary unit is the **dirham** (here: dh). In 1 dirham there are 100 **centimes**. Dirhams are very occasionally available at *bureaux de change* in London airports. As European Visa cards function in Moroccan ATMs (*guichets automatiques*), in major towns you can withdraw the amount you need each day. The euro is easily exchanged in the souks, as 10dh hovers around the €1 mark. Banking hours are usually 0830-1130 and 1500-1630, changing in summer and during Ramadan to 0830-1400. A budget traveller can get by for £23/€30, ie 300-400dh a day.

Security Marrakech and Essaouira are generally safe cities. The hassling of visitors has largely disappeared thanks to presence of the plain clothes *Brigade touristique*. However, watch belongings at bus and train stations. Off the beaten track in Marrakech or Safi, the worst that can happen is meeting the over-insistent neighbourhood nutter.

Telephone and internet All Moroccan numbers are nine digit, including the initial zero. Marrakech, Essaouira and Safi numbers begin 044, Oualidia numbers 023. Mobile numbers start 06 or 07. Calls can be made from the numerous *téléboutiques* in town centres. Cybercafés are centrally located – particularly Rue Bab Agnaou in Marrakech médina, or in Guéliz.

Vaccinations There is no malaria in Morocco. Take insect repellent as mosquitoes can be a nuisance. Your vaccinations for tetanus and polio should be up to date. In rural areas where hygiene is poor, vaccinations for hepatitis A and B are advisable.

Train

There is a good but slow train service to Marrakech from Morocco's major cities to the north run by the **ONCF** (Office national des chemins de fer), www.oncf.org.ma. If you can only get a flight to Casablanca, then it's worth thinking about taking the train to Marrakech. You will need to take the turquoise-blue Baydaoui shuttle train (*navette*) from Mohammed V airport to Casablanca Voyageurs station where you can pick up the main line service to Marrakech. There are five trains a day: generally two morning and two afternoon trains, plus a train in the small hours coming down from Tangiers. Prices on the railways are reasonable (first class has air conditioning). Generally, there is a trolley service with light refreshments. A first-class single ticket, Marrakech to Casa-Voyageurs is 110dh and the journey generally takes 3 hours.

Marrakech train station is generally heaving with people and taxi-touts. When leaving Marrakech, try to arrive at the station 30 minutes before departure. You can get a ticket-sized print-out of train times (*les horaires des trains pour Marrakech*) at the *guichet*. For train services to the Coast, see p30.

Getting around

Air

There are five daily RAM flights between Casablanca and Marrakech. (After a promising start in 2001, the Casablanca Mohammed V to Essaouira's Aéroport Mogador service has been discontinued.) In Casablanca, the main RAM can be reached on **T** 022-912000. RAM agencies: Marrakech, 197 Av Mohammed V, **T** 044-446444, **F** 044-446002; Casablanca, 44 Av des FAR, **T** 022-311122, **F** 022-442409. A single flight costs 850dh, a return 1,100dh.

Bus

Within Marrakech The city's pink and orange buses are clean and efficient. Tickets within the city are 3dh a ride. Line 1 runs from

from Arset el Bilk down Av Mohammed V to Guéliz. Line 7 does a similar route, but after Guéliz continues to Targa and the French Lycée Victor Hugo and the Institut Français. Line 8 runs from Arset el Bilk to Bab Doukkala (main bus station), then up to the ONCF rail station in Guéliz.

Atlantic coast destinations There are numerous buses from the *gare routière* at **Bab Doukkala**, **T** 044-435525, station to Essaouira (main bus-station **T** 044-475317), Safi and Oualidia. For Marrakech to Essaouira, however, prefer the **Supratours**, **T** 044-475317 service which leaves from next to the Marrakech rail station (turn right after you leave the station building) and arrives in the main square at Essaouira (fast and reliable journey time 1 hour 50 minutes). Like the Bab Doukkala bus station, Essaouira bus terminus is a bit of a zoo. There are a number of competing private companies running vehicles in various states of repair. As you enter the station building, touts come up to you to persuade you to opt for one company over another. Try to choose the one with the most reliable-looking vehicle. Timetables are not rigorously adhered to. After Supratours, the best bus company is the **CTM**, **T** 044-448328, www.ctm.co.ma. In Marrakech, the main CTM terminus is just down Boulevard Zerktouni from the Cinéma Colisée in Guéliz.

Car hire

Most of the main hire car companies are represented in Morocco (see Directory p214) and there are numerous small companies (reliability not always guaranteed). The smallest car available is the Fiat Uno, more rarely a Renault 4. Many agencies now have Fiat Palios in their fleets. The Peugeot 205 is felt to be a more reliable small car, with higher clearance and better road holding. A good deal would give you an Uno for 500dh a day, unlimited mileage, although certain Marrakech agencies (**Imzitours**, **T** 044-433934/36, imzi_tours@usa.net, for example) can be considerably cheaper. Note that many of the smaller agencies are just sub-contracting from the pool of vehicles in the city. Quality of service is hugely variable.

Four-wheel drives available in Morocco include the Suzuki Gemini (2 people) and the Vitara (4 people), at around 800dh per day; long-base Mitsubishi Pajeros (6 persons) are hired at 900dh to 1,000dh per day. Toyotas are said to be the best desert four-wheel drives. Landrovers are very uncomfortable for long cross-country runs on road, especially in summer without air conditioning. **NB** There is huge demand for hire cars during the Christmas and Easter breaks.

Cycling

Flat Marrakech was once a city with huge numbers of bicycles – now increasingly replaced by noisy mopeds. You can **rent bikes** by the hour, half-day or day from special stands near the Semlalia hotels (out on the Casablanca road, where there are some big hotels used by tour-groups; the bike hirer is in the open area, off the main road, where the coaches drop clients) or in the Hivernage (try next to the Hotel Siaha Safir), and near the Hotel Kenzi Farah. Great care should be taken when cycling, especially with careering mopeds. In places like Guéliz (near the Hotel Oudaïas and Jemaâ el Fna), there are bicycle and moped parks.

Taxis

Khaki-coloured **petits taxis** for up to three passengers are great for getting round Marrakech. Officially they are metered, with an initial minimum fare, followed by increments of time and distance although you may often find that there is no meter. There is a 50% surcharge after 2100. Drivers welcome a tip – many of them are not driving their own vehicles and make little more than 100dh a day. Short runs in Marrakech between médina and new town shouldn't cost much over 15dh during the day. After 2000 in winter and 2100 in summer taxi rates go up 50%. Note that only the big Mercedes taxis have the right to do runs out to the Palmeraie. Have change handy. Sometimes drivers take several passengers if they're headed in roughly the same direction especially from the train station.

Long distance **grands taxis**, generally Mercedes 200 saloon cars, run over fixed routes between cities, or within urban areas between centre and outlying suburbs. There is a fixed price for each route and passengers pay for a place, six in a Mercedes, nine in a Peugeot 504 estate car. Taxis wait until they are full. You may however, feel rich enough to pay for two places in order to be comfortable at the front (and be able to wear a safety belt). In a Peugeot estate, the best places are undoubtedly at the front, or, if you are quite small, right at the back. The middle place in the middle row is probably the worst option.

Between towns, grands taxis are quicker than trains or buses, and normally only a little more expensive. The main grand taxi rank in Marrakech is close to the Bab Doukkala bus station. In Essaouira and Safi, the intercity taxis leave from open ground next to the main bus stations. The principle is that drivers cry out the name of their destinations, and as you near the taxi station, you may be approached by touts eager to help you find a taxi. (This is especially true of Essaouira.) The standard of driving sometimes leaves a little to be desired.

In mountain areas, the same system applies, although the vehicles are Mercedes transit vans (where there is tarmac) or Landrovers, which have two people next to the driver and 10 in the back.

Train
There is no train service to Essaouira and there is no direct rail service to Safi from Marrakech, but you can get the main line service for Casablanca and change at Benguerir for the Safi branch line. The service is designed round the interests of the phosphate industry – morning departure from Safi to Benguerir (time 1 hour) is around 0815, afternoon departure from Benguerir is around 1700. A share-taxi is really the best option for doing the Marrakech to Safi run, second choice is the CTM bus (see above). Other bus services can be painfully slow.

Walking

Built on a plain, Marrakech is a city for walking, especially in the winter and spring. The train station is a 15-minute walk from the the central node of Guéliz, Rondpoint Abd el Moumen. From Guéliz to Jemaâ el Fna is a good 40-minute hike. The main bus station is at Bab Doukkala, on the west side of the médina and just 20 minutes walk from both Guéliz and Jemaâ el Fna. The médina is actually quite small – the Palace or Museum Quarter is 15 minutes' walk from Jemaâ el Fna, the Ben Youssef neighbourhood about 20 minutes. However, since there are lots of distractions and miscellaneous photo opportunities en route, walks in the médina tend to turn into rambles. (Happily there are lots of hole-in-the-wall *crèmerie* shops where you can sit down for a drink.) Both Essaouira and Safi are compact sorts of places. All the main sites can be covered in a half-day ramble. More time is necessary to get a feel for the atmosphere. For those with a yen for walking, the long windy beach at Essaouira is a big plus. For walking in the Atlas, see tours below and the High Atlas of Toubkal section starting on p65.

Tours and tourist information

Tours

Marrakech's main sites are in two areas, north and south of Jemaâ el Fna (the souks and Ben Youssef neighbourhood to the north, the Museum/Palace Quarter to the south). They are easily covered without a formal guide but if you want one it will cost you, say, 150-200dh for a half-day.

Official guides for walking tours around Marrakech can be contacted via the ONTM (see 'Tourist information' below) or one of the bigger hotels. Riad owners usually have someone to show guests around. Note that guides often like to take clients to carpet and souvenir shops were they get a percentage on any goods purchased. Be clear at the start of your city tour that time in carpet-bazaars is to be limited, unless you really want to buy a carpet. **Menara Tours**,

41 Rue Yougoslavie, **T** 044-446654, (English-speaking staff), runs day trips and is much used by English tour agencies.

To see something of the **High Atlas**, taking a four-wheel drive vehicle with driver or an organized four-wheel drive tour is a good option. Typical day trips include: the Kasbah of Telouet via the Tizi-n-Tichka (a long half day); Telouet, the kasbah-village of Aït ben Haddou, Ouarzazate and back (an exhausting full day); up the Ourika Valley to Setti Fatma on market day (half-day); up the Tizi-n-Test road to Ouirgane and the reconstructed medieval mosque at Tin Mal; into the High Atlas to Asni and Imlil; a four-wheel drive loop, up the Asni road and across to the Setti Fatma road, back via Dar Caïd Ourika. Costs vary, according to number of participants. Generally, in a four-wheel drive vehicle carrying six passengers, you'll be paying 350dh a head for a half-day excursion. Lunch, say 60dh, will be tajine at a roadside or market village restaurant. On a short break, best trips are Ouirgane/Tin Mal or Asni/Imlil, providing you can do a half-day walk to the village of Aremd near Imlil.

Based in Essaouira, **Sand Drifters**, BP 69 Essouira, Morocco 44000, **T** 0044-7906955428, 7792413971, www.sanddrifters.com, specialize in women-only travel to Morocco for independent travellers or groups. They find unusual accommodation and provide excellent local knowledge.

Atlas tour operators

There are a small number of reliable agencies who can set up day trips into the High Atlas. See also p221.

Atlas Sahara Trek, 6 bis Rue Houdhoud, Quartier Majorelle, **T** 044-313901, **F** 044-313905, sahara@cybernet.net.ma. Highly recommended agency with 18 years' experience of organizing treks in Morocco. Casablanca-born director Bernard Fabry knows the mountains well.

Atlas Voyages, 131 Blvd Mohammed V, **T** 044-430333, **F** 044-447185. Organizes a variety of excursions.

Complete Tours, Résidence Badr, 2nd floor, 220, Blvd

Mohammed V, Guéliz, **T** 06-1708036 (Tim Buxton). Works with a number of reputable British tour operators. Their Berber Trails four-wheel drive excursion is a firm favourite.

High Country, 31 Bab Amadil, Amizmiz, **T** 044-454847, highcountry@cybernet.net.ma. Agency based in Amizmiz in the foothills of the High Atlas. Organizes rock-climbing, off-roading, mountaineering, kayaking on the Lalla Takerkoust dam lake. Founded 1997, works with UK, US and Italian groups.

Pampa Voyages, Immeuble Jassim, 219 Blvd Mohammed V, Guéliz, **T** 044-431052, www.pampamaroc.com.

Tourist information

Marrakech   Marrakech has two tourist offices, both in Guéliz. The **ONTM** (*Office national du tourisme marocain*) is clearly visible on Place Abd el Moumen, near the Café Atlas, **T** 044-436131. *Opening hours are 0830-1200 and 1430-1830; 0900-1500 during Ramadan.* There is not much information available, apart from the standard issue glossy pamphlets. However, they can set up city visits with an official guide (standards variable). A half-day visit should be around 150dh, plus tip, 250dh for a full day. At 176 Av Mohammed V, almost opposite the Wafa Bank, is the second tourist information office, the **Syndicat d'Initiative**, **T** 044-432097/434797. Depending on who's on the desk, information is probably slightly better here.

Essaouira   **Syndicat d'Initiative**, Rue du Caire, **T** 044-475080. *Open (in principle) from 0900-1200 and 1500-1800. Hours vary, however.* Don't expect too much by way of useful information from this rather basic-looking office. In fact, they tend to send you to hotels which will pay them commission.

Safi   **ONTM**, Av de la Liberté, Ville Nouvelle. *Mon-Fri 0900-1200 and 1500-1830.* The Syndicat d'Initiative is near the *Hotel Assif*, too far from the main sites to be of much use. Though staff are friendly and willing to help, there is little Safi-specific information available.

High Atlas   No specific tourist information centres. The best place to pick up information on the mountains is probably the Hotel Ali, Rue Moulay Ismaïl, off Jemaâ el Fna in Marrakech. Trekking guides hang out here and reception will put you in contact with someone.

Maps

Of the road maps of Morocco, the Michelin map, sheet 959, scale 1:4,000,000 is probably the best (insets of certain areas). Hiking maps of the High Atlas are produced by the Division de la Cartographie, Av Hassan II, Rabat, **T** 037-705311. The *Hotel Ali* generally has a small stock of these government-produced maps. Use the following three 1:100,000 scale maps: **Tizi-n-Test** (NH-29-XVI-4), **Toubkal** (NH-29-XXIII-1) and **Amizmiz** (NH-29-XXII-2).

In London, **Stanfords** at 12-14 Long Acre, Covent Garden, WC2E 9LP, **T** 020-78361321, www.stanfords.co.uk, has a pack of four maps for the Toubkal region, including Amizmiz, Oukaïmeden-Toubkal, the Tizi-n-Test and Taliouine.

The newspaper kiosk next to the tourist office on Rondpoint Abd el Moumen carries a range of Marrakech city maps. The best maps of Essaouira are in the freebie tourist publications.

Marrakech

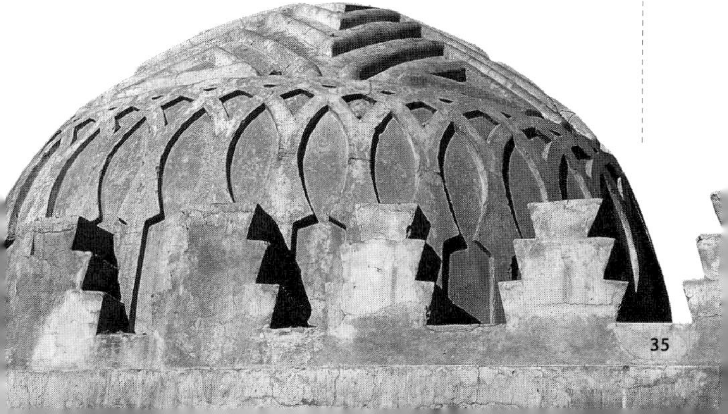

Jemaâ el Fna and around 37 The vivid heart of Marrakech, pulsating soundscape, crossroads for cosmopolitans and locals. A road movie sort of urban space.

Northern médina 42 A labyrinth of souks traditional and tawdry. A historic Islamic college, Morocco-Baroque restaurants, the ancient Almoravid dome and festering vats of the tanneries.

South of Jemaâ el Fna: the 'Palace Quarter' 50 Bygone splendours of vanished dynasties. Palaces with jungle courtyards play home to craft collections. An urban olive grove at the Agdal gardens.

The walls and gates 57 Take a carriage ride to view the city's earth-red fortifications, testimony to an 11th-century warrior dynasty.

Guéliz and Hivernage and the gardens 59 Modern city and garden suburb. Chic shopping and reasonably-priced licensed restaurants. Top hotels and nightspots on tree-lined avenues.

Jemaâ el Fna and around

*Beating heart of Marrakech, the sprawling 'square' of Jemaâ el Fna is both the city's greatest tourist draw and still a genuine social hub for the Marrakchis. On a médina map, Jemaâ el Fna, aka 'la Place' figures as an irregular space in the middle of the médina. It is far more. Each hour of the day has its own character. In the morning, things are quiet – the area looks like nothing so much as an empty car park. By midday, the street entertainers are in action and camcorders are whirring. By mid-afternoon, the square is full of people hawking talents and goods, bystanders gawping, walking, talking and arguing. Activity ends late at night when barbecue stalls and the last musician have packed up. Jemaâ el Fna is particularly memorable during Ramadan when the day's fast ends. But whatever the time of day or year, you will return to 'la Place' again and again, responding to its magnetic pull, to mingle with the crowd or watch the jostle from the terraces of the **Café de France** or the **Café Argana**. Nearby, dominating Marrakech's skyline looms the towering minaret of the **Koutoubia Mosque**, another important focal point and landmark. Running into Jemaâ el Fna from the southwest is the pedestrian **Rue Bab Agnaou**, packed in the early evening with strollers. And off the north side of the square is the small **Place Bab Fteuh**. Its old merchant hostels will delight junk fanatics.*
▸▸ *See Sleeping p103, Eating and drinking p130*

◉ Sights

★ Place Jemaâ el Fna
Open 24 hours, liveliest from 1600-2100, later in summer.
Map 3, D6/7, p252

'Jemaâ el Fna is not what it was', old Marrakchis moan. Back before Independence, 'la Place' was ankle-deep in dust in summer and a sea of mud after the winter rains. The idea was even mooted that the area should be used as building land. Until the late 1980s, the city bus station was on the Jemaâ, a chaos of ramshackle charabancs and Mercedes taxis. Things have been cleaned up a lot since then. In 1994, for the GATT meeting, the tarmac spreaders were brought in and the juice barrows and barbecue stands got numbers. The dust is a thing of the past – careering vélomoteurs are more of a problem. And there are dark rumours of a mini-mall complex on the Riad Zitoun side.

Take time to wander round 'la Place'. Amateur apothecaries spread out their herbs and unguents on sacking, offering advice on problems of fertility and virility, possibly alarm-clocks, miscellanous CDs and the odd mummified reptile; there are snake charmers and monkey tamers, watersellers and wildly grinning gnaoua musicians with giant metal castanets, all too ready for photographers. Sheltering from the sun under their umbrellas, the fortune tellers and public scribes await their clients.

In the evening, the crowd changes again, a mix of students and people pausing on the way home from work, smart tourists strolling to exclusive patio restaurants in the médina, and backpackers ready for hot tagine or harira soup at one of the foodstalls. You may see Ouled el Moussa tumblers or a storyteller enthralling the crowd. Sometimes there are boxers and almost always groups of musicians. After much effort to extract a few dirhams from the crowd, an acoustic band will get some Amazigh dancing. More moving are the groups performing songs by the activist groups popular in the 1970s, Jil Jilala and Nass el Ghiwane. (Every Moroccan knows a song or two by these bands.) There may be *nakkachat*, women with syringes full of henna, ready to pipe a design onto your hands, as if they were decorating a cake. Modern

! Who knows the meaning of Jemaâ el Fna? In classical Arabic, *jemaâ* suggests a gathering, while *fna* means open space – and ruin, annihilation, and obliteration of the self (in the mystic tradition). Some say the square is named on account of the executed criminals' heads displayed there in former times.

Jemaâ el Fna
'La Place': the thrumming, humming heart of Marrakech.

innovations include a fairground game of 'hook the ring over the coke bottle', while a lad with a dumb-bell improvised from two old millstones will let you do some exercises for a dirham or two. You may find an astrologist-soothsayer tracing out his diagram of the future on the tarmac with a scrubby piece of chalk. A modern variation on the traditional *halka* or storyteller's circle touches harsh social reality: local people listen to a true tale told with dignity by the relatives of a victim of poverty or injustice. And should you need an aphrodisiac, there are stalls with tea urns selling cinnamon and ginseng tea and little dishes of black, powdery *slilou*, a spicy sweet paste.

Remember: watch your wallet and have change handy for entertainers and orange juice. There shouldn't be any hassle as the plain-clothes Brigade Touristique is watching, and penalties for bothering visitors are severe.

Koutoubia Mosque
The mosque is only open to Muslims. Map 3, E4, p252

As the Eiffel Tower is to Paris, so the 65-metre high minaret of the Koutoubia Mosque is to Marrakech. Visible from afar, it is the landmark which was to be the focal point for urban planner Henri Prost when he laid out the modern neighbourhood of Guéliz. Unlike many mosques in Morocco's old cities, it is readily approachable, being surrounded by an esplanade and rose gardens. The name Koutoubia derives from the Arabic *kutoub* (books) and means the 'Booksellers' Mosque'. No doubt the noble business of selling manuscripts was conducted in a souk close to the mosque.

Unusually, the Koutoubia is a double mosque, both parts dating from the reign of the second Almohad ruler, Abd el Moumen (1130-63). Standing on the esplanade facing the minaret, the ruins of the first Koutoubia are behind railings to your right (first excavated in the late 1940s, and re-explored recently). The bases of the prayer hall's columns, and the cisterns under the courtyard, are clearly visible. The ground plan of the second Koutoubia, still standing, is the same as that of the ruined one (17 naves). (The Almohad mosque at Tin Mal, visitable for non-Muslims, has a similar plan, see p69.)

So why, back in the 12th century, did the Almohads go to the trouble of building not one but two mosques? Why bother destroying the Almoravid mosque? The site of the mosque is itself historic, having been originally occupied by a late 11th-century kasbah, the Almoravid Dar el Hajar (lit. 'House of Stone'). The victorious Almohads destroyed much of the Almoravid city they found. In 1147 they built a large mosque, close to the Dar el Hajar fortress. This they had to do, as no Almohad would pray in a

! For a close-up view of the top of the mosque and its *darj wa ktaf*, 'step-and-shoulder' design feature, consult your 100dh banknote.

building put up by the heretic Almoravids. Unfortunately, the orientation of the new Almohad mosque was not quite right – the focal point in a mosque, indicated by the mihrab, or prayer niche, should be in the direction of Mecca. The solution was to build a second mosque – the present Koutoubia – even though the faithful at prayer can correct this directional problem themselves, under the direction of the imam.

Thus two mosques existed for some time side by side, the first probably functioning as a sort of annexe (and given Almohad religious fervour, congregations were no doubt large). Today, the bricked-up spaces on the northwest wall of the Koutoubia Mosque indicate the doors which connected them. However, the total complex was perhaps excessive in size and the older structure eventually fell into ruin.

The existing Koutoubia Mosque was built by Abd el Moumen in 1162. The minaret, an impressive feat of engineering in its day, was to influence subsequent buildings in Morocco. It culminates in a ribbed dome topped with three golden orbs, allegedly made from the melted down jewellery of Sultan Yacoub el Mansour's wife, in penance for her having eaten three grapes during Ramadan.

A vast structure for its day, the Koutoubia is held to be the high point of Almohad art, a cathedral-mosque of classic simplicity. It is here that the innovations of Hispano-Moorish art – stalactite cupolas, painted wooden ceilings – reach perfection. There are perspectives of horseshoe arches, no doubt an aid to contemplation. (Although the prayer hall is off limits to the non-Muslim visitor, an idea of what it is like can be gained at the Tin Mal mosque in the High Atlas.) The unique *minbar* (preacher's chair) can be seen in the Badi Palace and is all decoration and variety, a sharp contrast to the austerity of the prayer hall. Ultimately, the Koutoubia is striking because it is the work of one ruler, Abd el Moumen. Comparable buildings in western Islam – the Great Mosque of Cordoba and the Alhambra – were built over a couple of centuries.

● *West of the Koutoubia is a splendid rose garden from where you will get the best views of the minaret. Pass through here on your way to take a squint at the legendary Hotel Mamounia.*

Northern médina

North of 'la Place' lie the **souks** *of Marrakech, the old city's beating commercial heart. Tides of locals and tourists flow through the vibrant covered alleys, stuffed with every variety of merchandise, from the traditionally seductive to the electrically Taiwanese. There are streets filled with every variety of soft slipper, jellaba and kelim. Pottery ranges from twinkly bibelots to clan-sized oil-jars. In another souk, the vendors peer over baskets overflowing with dates, nuts and dried figs. The stalls of* **Souk el Ghazal** *are steeped in superstition: the raw materials for spells – chameleons, blackbird heads, powders and unguents – are here obtainable.*

North of the souks, in the **Ben Youssef neighbourhood**, *sits a clutch of important historic buildings. The domed* **Almoravid Koubba** *is the city's oldest building. Nearby is the former* **Dar Mnebhi**, *now housing the collections of the Musée de Marrakech. Further on, the* **Medersa Ben Youssef** *is where, in the not so very distant past, students assimilated Islamic learning. Courtyard and oratory are high points of Maghrebi building. The* **Dar Belarj**, *the 'house of the stork' hosts occasional contemporary art shows.*

A 10-minute walk from the Ben Youssef area, the traditional **tanneries** *at Bab Debbagh are not an 'attraction' for the faint-hearted. Down a series of dusty lanes, through a low door lie scenes of frenetic medieval industry. Lads haul and tread skins in vats of evil-smelling liquid and the processes of leather-making are enacted before your eyes. And almost as compelling as the tanneries is the street life of the area: kids and their kick-arounds, the mint seller, the mule-carts, the overspill of workshop activity into the alleys.*

▸▸ *See Sleeping p106, Eating and drinking p106, Arts and Entertainment p157, Shopping p173*

◉ Sights

Souks

Open daily. Fri early closing, about 1130. Not everybody opens in the evening. During Ramadan, hours are more erratic: smaller stalls open late and close about an hour before sundown. Map 3, A/C 7/8, p252

Once upon a time, each of the covered market streets of central Marrakech was devoted to a specific craft. Although many of the original functions have gone, the souks have a real buzz. Encouraged by the influx of artsy residents from Europe, the craftsmen have adapted their skills to producing lamps and chests, textiles and bibelots of every shape and size. Alongside tiny stalls, there are emporia where haute decoration rules. Souking is not a relaxing experience – traders besiege visitors with pleas of 'just for looking' or similar. Get an idea of prices before choosing a shop and getting down to serious bargaining. Experiences with unofficial guides vary. They can be more trouble and expense than they're worth – or prove extremely helpful in negotiating the maze of streets. **NB** Don't believe the 'Buy now, Berber market only open today' line. The phrase can be heard every day.

The most obvious way in is to the left of the mosque almost opposite the Café de France. Follow the street round to the left and then turn right into the main thoroughfare, **Souk Semmarine**. Alternatively, enter through the small tourist pottery market, further round to the left on Jemaâ el Fna. Souk Semmarine is a busy place, originally the textiles market, and although there are a number of large, expensive tourist shops, there are still some cloth sellers. To the left is a covered *kissaria* selling clothes. The first turning on the right takes you past a right turn for **Souk Larzal**, once a wool market, to **Rahba Kedima**, (lit. 'the old square'). Here you now find traditional cures and cosmetics, spices, vegetables and cheap jewellery. There are also a couple of good carpet emporia, easily identified by the bright red and orange rugs hanging on the shopfronts. Walk back onto the main souk via a short alley with wood-carved goods. Here the main drag is called **Souk el Attarine** (if you turn left) or **Souk el Kebir** (if you turn right).

Head up Souk el Kebir. The first right takes you to an area called the **Criée berbère** where slaves, brought mainly from West Africa, were auctioned until 1912. Back on Souk el Kebir, heading northwards, you reach a stretch of street called the **Souk des Bijoutiers**. The main drag begins to narrow. To the left is a network of small alleys, the *kissarias*, selling mass-produced goods, beyond or west of which is the **Souk Cherratine**, with leather goods, somewhere to bargain for camel or cowhide bags, purses and belts. However, if you follow Souk el Kebir/the main route through, you'll reach an open space, the start of the Ben Youssef neighbourhood. Here you're close to a small concentration of must-see historic buildings, including the Almoravid Koubba, the Musée de Marrakech and the Medersa Ben Youssef.

Almoravid Koubba (Koubba el Ba'diyine)
0900-1300 and 1430-1800. 10dh. Map 3, A8, p253

Protected by elaborate neo-Versailles iron railings, the Almoravid Koubba (lit. the Almoravid dome, also referred to as Koubba el Ba'diyine) is a rare architectural survival from the 12th century. Dating from the reign of Ali Ben Youssef (1107-43), it is the only complete Almoravid building. Originally, it would have been an ablutions block for the now vanished neighbouring mosque.

At first glance the koubba seems a simple affair, basically a square stone and brick structure topped with a dome. However, take in the elaborate interlocking designs, and the arches leading into the koubba which are different on each side. Climb down the stairs to see inside, neckache guaranteed as you view the fossilized spider's web of patterns under the dome. Features include an octagon within an eight-pointed star, plus motifs typical of the period, including the palmette, pine cone and acanthus. Around

Almoravid Koubba

Ancestor of Gothic? Rediscovered in the 20th century, the bulky Almoravid Koubba maintains a presence in the Ben Youssef neighbourhood.

the corniche is a dedicatory inscription. The basin in the floor would have been used for ablutions – face, arm and feet washing being obligatory for Muslims before prayer.

Musée de Marrakech

Place Ben Youssef, **T** 044-390911/12. *0900-1800, closed Mon. 30dh. After the entrance courtyard (good café and clean loos on left, ticket office and bookshop on right), a narrow corridor takes you into the exhibition areas proper. Map 3, A9, p253*

With its post-modern crenellations, the entrance to the Musée de Marrakech is clearly in evidence just off the open area in front of the Almoravid Koubba. The museum is housed in Dar M'nebhi, the early 20th-century palace of a former Moroccan minister of war. The domestic wing hosts occasional displays of contemporary art. Over the main courtyard, now entirely paved and covered with a plexiglass roof hovers a brass chandelier as big as a small UFO. Here you'll find displays of manuscripts, coins, ceramics and textiles. Note the Portuguese influence in the carved wooden fronting for the rooms on the left. A small passageway to the left of the main reception room takes you through to the restored hammam, now home to a collection of early Moroccan engravings.

Mosque and Medersa Ben Youssef
Pl Ben Youssef. *0900-1200, 1430-1800, closed Fri. Map 3, A8/9, p253*

Standing with the Almoravid Koubba behind you, the minaret of the large 12th-century Ben Youssef Mosque, rebuilt in the 19th century, is clearly visible. Turning right out of the Museé de Marrakech, follow the street round and you will come to the entrance of the 16th-century Medersa Ben Youssef. One of the few Islamic buildings open to the general public, it was recently restored by the Fondation Ben Jelloun. Founded in 1564-65 by the Saâdian Sultan Moulay Abdallah, on the site of a previous Merinid medersa, it was within recent memory still a boarding school for students of the religious sciences and law. The medersa centres on a square courtyard containing a rectangular pool, and with arcades on two sides. Students shared the tiny rooms, each with a sleeping loft and a window looking onto the courtyard. Weathered carved cedar wood covers the upper part of the courtyard façades. Up to eye level, there is *zellige* tiling on the walls and pillars. Around the courtyard flows a frieze of calligraphed inscriptions.

At the far end of the courtyard is the prayer hall, covered with an

! In the médina, you'll see kids carrying trays of homemade round loaves to the neighbourhood oven. Sometimes the oven is dual-purpose, baking bread and heating the water of the local hammam.

eight-sided wooden dome. Light pierces the gloom through small windows screened with plaster open-work. In the qibla wall is a five-sided mihrab with a dedication to the pious sultan Abdallah, 'the most glorious of all caliphs'. Note the stalactite ceiling of the mihrab, and the carved stucco walls with pine cone motif. (Why did they go for pine cones?)

Dar Belarj

Place Ben Youssef, **T** 044-444555. *Daily 0900-1800. 15dh.*
Map 2, H9, p251

Turning right out of the medersa, then left along a covered street, you will come to the entrance of Dar Belarj, 'the House of Storks', on your left. Take a look in here if you have plenty of time – mint tea is available. Dating from the 1930s, the building was restored by a couple of Swiss artists in the late 1990s. Prior to this there was a fondouk on the site which housed the only hospital for birds in North Africa. Here there dwelt a wise man who had the gift of curing wounded storks. Unfortunately, austerely refurbished Dar Belarj no longer has any red-beaked residents and it's really only worth a look if there is an exhibition or event. If director Susan Biederman is on hand she may have time to explain the house and its restoration.

Fondouks in the Ben Youssef area

Rue Souk Ahl Fass. 0800-late afternoon. No activity Fri afternoon. No official admission price. Map 3, A8, p253

East of the Medersa Ben Youssef, a street known as the the Souk of the Fassis runs east, turning into Rue Debbagh as it approaches the tanneries located inside the city's eastern wall. On the Fassi souk stretch are at a number of old merchants' hostelries, for this was the city's original hotel district. There would have been stabling for mules on the ground floor, accommodation upstairs off the galleries. The fondouks (an Arabic term derived from the Greek *pandokeion* meaning hostelry), as these courtyard buildings are called, are now home to small-scale craft enterprises, producing all manner of articles for the souks. A look in here gives you an idea of the tough conditions in which men (and boys) labour to produce those bijou decorative must-haves.

● *One of the hostels has been refurbished in Afro-minimalist taste to become the restaurant Le Fondouk, see p135. It could be worth a stop on your way to the tanneries.*

Tanneries near Bab Debbagh
0800-1400. No activity Fri afternoon. No official admission price. Perhaps worth a donation of 20-30dh to whoever takes you round? Map 2, H1, p251

'Bab Debbagh, bab deheb' – 'Tanners' Gate, gold gate' – the old adage goes, in reference to the tanners' prosperity. They are said to have been the first people to settle in Marrakech at its foundation and the fact that they have a gate named after them, the only one to be named for a craft corporation, bears this out. The tanneries are certainly worth a look, especially if you have a yen for discovering the nitty-gritty of the pre-industrial process in full operation. (Try to get a view of the area from the leather shop terrace next to Bab Debbagh.) If you are in the Ben Youssef area, you will in all likelihood be approached by some lad who will offer to show you the tanneries (who will of course expect a tip, see above).

Through a small metal door, you will be shown an area of foul-smelling pits, where men tread and rinse skins in nauseously pungent liquid – all just a meander away from bijou riads and palaces. In small lean-to buildings, you will find other artisans scraping and stretching the skins. Located close to the seasonal Oued Issil and on the edge of the city, the tanners originally had plenty of water and space to expand away from residential areas. The tannery was considered a dangerous place as it was the entrance to the domain of the 'Other Ones' (djinn). It was also a beneficial one, since skins symbolized preservation and fertility. Bab Debbagh was the eastern gate into the city, and there was a symbolism based on the sun rising in the east and skin being reborn as leather. The tanners, because they spent their days in pits working the skins, were said to be in contact with the unseen world of the dead; they were also seen as masters of fertility, being strong men, capable of giving a second life to dry, dead skin.

In the old days, the complex process of tanning would start with soaking the skins in a sort of swamp – or *iferd* – in the middle of the tannery, filled with a fermenting mixture of pigeon guano and tannery waste. This is followed by a process of soaking the skins in various mixtures of ash and lime, guano (again) and finally chaff and salt, to remove all flesh and hair. Only then can the actual tanning process begin. (The word *debbagh* actually means tannin.) After this, the skins are prepared for dyeing.

In Marrakech, you will probably be told that there are two tanneries: one Arab, the other Berber. In all likelihood, the workforce is ethnically mixed today. Certainly there are specialities, with one set of tanners working mainly on the more difficult cow and camel skins, and the others on goat and sheep skins. For the record, the tanners were known to be great nocturnal hunters, doing a trade in hedgehog skins for magic. They were also known as big kif smokers: working in such difficult conditions with the foul odours and the presence of spirits would have been difficult without a daily pipe of *kif*.

● *If walking precariously between pools of slimy skins and sludge proves too much for you, you can always take a carriage to one of Marrakech's nearby gardens, see p59.*

! Take the *djinn* seriously. They live deserted places, hammams, wells and water pipes. In a Marrakchi kitchen, boiling water is never poured down a sink for fear of scalding 'the Other Ones'. Usually invisible, the *djinn* sometimes take on animal shape.

South of Jemaâ el Fna

*The great museum-palaces of Marrakech lie south of Jemaâ el Fna. With its wider, straighter streets, this area is easier to negotiate than the labyrinthine northern médina. From 'la place', Riad Zitoun el Kedim leads down to a confusing junction and the Place des Ferblantiers, home to the metal workers. Through a gate, down a giant-sized corridor between pisé walls is the entrance to the **El Badi Palace**. All that remains of a 16th-century golden sultan's greatest palace is a vast precinct set with sunken orange groves. The rooftops of the present royal palace complex lie just beyond.*

*A confusing ramble away, not far from Bab Agnaou, behind the Kasbah Mosque, high walls hide a masterpiece of Moorish architecture, the **Saâdian Mausoleum**. Carved stucco traceries arch over the marble tombs of 17th-century princelings. Poetically lost to the world for a couple of centuries, this jewel box of a monument was only rediscovered in the early 20th century.*

*Another street running south of Jemaâ el Fna, Riad Zitoun el Jedid, takes you to more palatial homes turned over to cultural display. The **Dar Si Saïd** houses the city's biggest collection of Moroccan traditional arts and crafts: rare carpets, pottery and all manner of rural implements. Nearby, the **Bahia Palace** is a mosaic of fountain courtyards and cool, high-ceilinged chambers. One-time home of a cruel vizier, droves of tourists now pass through. Look in at the **Maison Tiskiwine**, a modest home containing a unique private collection of Moroccan textiles.*

▸▸ See Sleeping p108, Eating and drinking p137

◉ Sights

Kasbah Mosque
Not open to non-Muslims. Map 3, H6, p252

The road from Bab Agnaou leads to Rue de la Kasbah, turn right along here and then take the first left. On this road is the much-

Bab Agnaou
Horse-shoe arched gate, declaring architecturally that you are entering a most imperial city.

restored Kasbah Mosque, dating from 1190. The minaret has Almohad *darj wa ktaf* (step and shoulder) and *shabka* (net) motifs on alternate sides, all on a background of green tiles. Though not as impressive as the tower of the Koutoubia Mosque, the minaret is a notable landmark en route to the Saâdian Tombs.

Saâdian Tombs
0800-1200, 1400-1800, generally closed Tue. 10dh. The entrance lies directly to the right of the Kasbah mosque. Map 1, G9, p249

French archaeologists and savants had a field day in early 20th-century Morocco: here was an exotic land, untouched by modernity, ripe for study. The Saâdian Tombs must rate as one of their more exciting discoveries, a high point in Islamic art. How did the mausolea escape the destructive rage of Sultan Moulay Ismaïl, he who set out to destroy all traces of the Saâdians? Perhaps sealing off the tombs was the best way to consign the dynasty to oblivion – without profaning what was after all a royal burial place. Whatever, the Saâdian rulers' last resting place is a Moorish architectural bijou – 'discovered' in 1917 thanks to aerial photography. Access had been via the neighbouring mosque, so a corridor had to be created to give non-Muslim visitors access to the two mausolea. In the first, the *mihrab* (prayer niche) of the first main burial chamber is particularly impressive. Here lies Prince Moulay Yazid. In the second room is buried the great Ahmed al Mansour, 'the Golden', surrounded by his sons. A third, more poignant chamber contains children's graves. The second mausoleum contains the tombs of Ahmed al Mansour's mother, the venerated Lalla Messaouda, and Mohammed Ech Cheikh, founder of the Saâdians. Overall, the mausolea are not so very different from the private chapel of a European noble family.

● *Visit early in the day. Later the dignity and repose of the Saâdians gets a little ruffled by tour groups.*

El Badi Palace
0900-1200 and 1430-1730 (closed during the two Aïd holidays). 10dh. Map 3, H7, p253

El Badi Palace was built by the Saâdian Sultan Ahmed al Mansour ed-Dahbi (the Golden) between 1578 and 1593, following his accession after his victory over the Portuguese at the Battle of the Three Kings, at Ksar el Kebir in northern Morocco. To get there coming from 'la Place' down Riad Zitoun el Kedim, head onto Place des Ferblantiers (a square with workshops turning out tin lanterns etc), then turn right once though the big gate in the wall and you'll find the 'corridor' between massive walls leading to the palace.

The 16th-century palace marks the height of Saâdian power, the centrepiece of an imperial capital. It was a lavish display of the best craftsmanship of the period, using the most expensive materials, including gold, marble and onyx. Today only the great walls have survived as a reminder of one of the periodic royal re-foundations of

Marrakech. The palace was largely destroyed in the 17th century by Moulay Ismaïl, who stripped it of its decorations and fittings and carried them off to Meknès. No austere royal fortress, the Badi was probably a palace for audiences – and it was at one of these great court ceremonies that the building's fate was predicted: "Among the crowds taking part at the banquet was a visionary who, at the time, enjoyed a certain reputation for his saintliness. 'What do you think of this palace?' asked the Sultan Al Mansour in jest. 'When it is demolished, it will make a big pile of earth', replied the visionary. Al Mansour was lost for words at this answer. He felt a sinister omen." (El Ifrani, a historian writing in the early 18th century also noted the inauspicious numerical meaning of the palace's name. The value of its letters is 117 – exactly the number of lunar years the palace remained intact: from 1002 AH to 1119 AH, that is 1594-1708.)

The name El Badi ties in with the palace's once elaborate decoration. In Arabic, *ilm el badi* is one of the main varieties of classical Arabic rhetoric, the art of stylistic ornament – and the palace was certainly one of the most decorated in its day. Above one of the main gates, the following inscription was placed in flowing Arabic calligraphy: "This gate is as beautiful as the eloquent beginning of a fine poem, and the palace is as the continuation of this poem. Thus it was named Badi, using hyperbole, assonance and pleonasm."

In its day, the Badi Palace was the physical symbol of the Golden Sultan's glory. Al Mansour had conquered the Sudan (Arabic for 'blacks'), bringing them under Islamic rule. Deeply influenced by Ottoman court traditions, he no doubt hoped to establish the imposing ceremonial of the Istanbul court in Morocco. The palace drew in wealth and skilled craftsmen from all over. The colonnades were of marble, apparently bought, or rather exchanged with Italian merchants, for their equivalent weight in sugar. Al Mansour had sugar-cane presses built. Perhaps there is a visual message here, the power of the prince transforming crystalline sugar into white marble and stucco. Sugary sweets were distributed to the

Sultan's guests – at a time when well-refined sugar was a rarity. The ill omens which had so frightened Al Mansour were realized: not only was the palace destroyed, but all its fine building materials were dispersed. The glory of the palace was dismantled, and in the words of one contemporary observer, "there was not a single city in Morocco which did not receive some debris of El Badi." The vaulting ambition and power of the great Moulay Ismaïl in turn had to find an expression in stone – or rather adobe – walls, but at Meknès, not Marrakech. Perhaps there was a political logic to all this building activity. Moulay Ismaïl is said to have declared: "If I have a sack full of rats, I must move the sack constantly to prevent them from escaping."

In July, El Badi comes alive each weekend for the annual festival of traditional dance and music. Films are screened here in late September for the *Festival du film de Marrakech*. Most of the year, however, the palace enclosure is a quiet sort of place, the high thick walls protecting the vast courtyard from the noise of the surrounding streets. The courtyard is divided by water channels connecting a number of pools. The largest of these even has an island. The ruins on either side of the courtyard were probably summer houses, the one at the far end being called the Koubba el Khamsiniya after the 50 pillars in its construction. The complex contains a small museum which includes the movable *minbar*, a sort of pulpit, from the Koutoubia Mosque. The scattered ruins of the palace, with odd fragments of decoration amidst the debris, also include stables and dungeons.

Dar Si Saïd
Rue de la Bahia. *0900-1200 and 1430-1745, closed Tue and public holidays. 20dh. Map 3, F9, p253*

To get to the southeast area of the médina follow Rue des Banques from just past Café de France on the Jemaâ el Fna. This leads into Riad Zitoun Jedid. Off to the left is the Dar Si Saïd, a palatial

▶ His Majetski, King of the Poor

Morocco's king, Mohammed VI, is a popular sort of chap. Soon after coming to the throne in July 1999, he was dubbed M6 (pronounced *'em-six'*, as in French). For his visits to the poorest bidonvilles and the remotest parts of the country, places where his father, the redoubtable Hassan II, would never set foot, he quickly earned himself another nickname: *le roi des pauvres*. Right from the start of the reign, pressing the flesh became part of the royal repertoire. Today, the monarch's amenable, slightly chubby features are everywhere. On boulevard billboards, he appears in formal white robes – or else in shades and military fatigues. Government offices display pictures of a be-suited, executive Majesty, while shops prefer the casual photos: the King in ski-gear, or with a wooly gnaoua cap in Rasta colours atop the royal bonce, or even breaking the waves on a jet-ski. (His liking for this sport earned him a further title: *Sa Majetski*.) Concerned for the poor he may be, but the King is also *wa'er* – seriously trendy. In summer 2002, M6 increased his popularity by marrying an ordinary, but stunning, Fès girl, now Princess Lalla Selma (also a computer engineer). In May 2003, an heir was born, Crown Prince Hassan. So, provided the country's technocratic governments can deliver jobs and prosperity, Morocco's monarchy seems set to carry on in public life.

complex originally built by Si Saïd, vizier under Moulay El Hassan, and half-brother of Ba Ahmed. Today it houses the Museum of Moroccan Arts and Crafts. The collections include pottery, jewellery, leatherwork from Marrakech and Chichaoua carpets. Amazigh artifacts, (daggers, copperware, jewellery of silver, ivory and amber) are one of its strongpoints. The first floor has been made into an elegant salon with Hispano-Moorish decoration. In a cool and pleasant courtyard, a remarkable collection of old window and door frames is on display. Items to look out for include a marble basin, unusually decorated with heraldic birds, from Islamic Spain, and a primitive four-seater wooden ferris wheel of the type still found in *moussems* (country fairs) in Morocco.

● *Those particularly interested in traditional Moroccan artefacts will want to continue to the neighbouring Maison Tiskiwine.*

Maison Tiskiwine

8 Rue de la Bahia, **T** 044-443335. *0930-1230 and 1500-1830. 15dh.*
Map 3, F9, p253

Between the Palace and Dar Si Said is the Maison Tiskiwine ('the House of the Horns'), a modest courtyard house which is home to a fine array of items related to Moroccan rural society. The collection was assembled over a lifetime in Morocco by Dutch art historian and Marrakech resident Bert Flint. There is an exhibition of craftsmen's materials and techniques from regions as far apart as the Rif, High Atlas and the Sahara, including jewellery and costumes, musical instruments, carpets and furniture. Flint was also instrumental in setting up another collection of traditional Moroccan craftwork for the City Council in Agadir.

Bahia Palace

Riad Zitoun el Jedid, **T** 044-389564. *Mon-Thu 0830-1145, 1430-1745, Sat and Sun 0830-1130 and 1500-1745, closed Fri. 10dh.*
Map 3, G10, p253

Further to the south is the Bahia Palace (Bahia means 'brilliant'). It was built in the last years of the 19th century by the vizier Ba Ahmed ben Moussa, or Bou Ahmed, a former slave who exercised considerable power under Sultans Moulay Hassan and Abd el Aziz. Generally packed with tour groups, the palace is a maze of corridors, passageways and empty chambers with painted ceilings. The story goes that Bou Ahmed was so hated that, on his death in 1900, his palace was looted and his possessions stolen by slaves, servants and members of his harem. The visit concludes with a marble paved courtyard of 50x30 m, and the guides will tell you that each wife and concubine had a room looking onto the patio. The French authorities set up shop here when they occupied Marrakech in the early 1900s, installing all manner of mod cons. With the pleasant garden courtyards and high cedarwood ceilinged chambers, you can easily see why.

The Jewish quarter (Mellah)
Map 3, H10, p253

The mellah was created in 1558. This lies south of the Bahia Palace and to the west of the El Badi Palace. It's an extensive quarter reflecting the Jewish community's historic importance to the city, when they were involved in the sugar trade and banking, as well as providing most of the jewellers, metalworkers and tailors. There were several synagogues and, under the control of the community's rabbis, the area had considerable autonomy. Few Jews remain today, the last wave of departures happening after the 1973 war, and the quarter's once-distinct feel has all but vanished. The synagogues have been closed and their paraphernalia removed to Israel or elsewhere. There is a small, plain synagogue visited by Jewish tourists down an alley as you face the restaurant Dar Douiria, which is on your right as you leave the Place des Ferblantiers behind you when you leave the Palais Badi. Don't expect to knock and find anyone automatically there to show you around.

The walls and gates

The Red City's 16 km of ramparts, set with 20 gates and 200 towers date from Almoravid times (11th century) – excepting those around the

Agdal Gardens which are more recent. Packed earth being a crumbly sort of material, there has been much reconstruction down the centuries. A popular way to see something of the ramparts is a ride in a horse-drawn calèche. In places, there has been much beautification going on of late on the western side of town, with fancy wrought iron railings and rose gardens taking the place of dusty wasteland.

◉ Sights

Around the gates
See also Bab Debbagh and the tanneries, p48.

Bab Rob, near the buses and grands taxis on the southwest side of the médina, is Almohad, and is named after the grape juice which could only be brought through this gate. **Bab Debbagh** (the Tanners' gate), on the east side, is an intricate defensive gate with a twisted entrance route and wooden gates, which could shut off the various parts of the building for security. From the top of the gate there would be a good view of the tanneries if one were allowed up. Note that hides are often laid out to dry on the banks of the nearby Oued Issil – where a large social housing development is going up, replacing the local bidonville. **Bab el Khemis**, on the northeast side, opens into the Souk el Khemis (Thursday market) and an important area of mechanics and craftsmen. Stop in to check out the junk-market on a Sunday morning. There is a small saint's tomb inside the gate building. **Bab Doukkala**, on the northwest side by the bus station, is a large gate with a horseshoe arch and two towers. Occasional art exhibitions have been held inside. The esplanade in front of the gate is being revamped. Close to the bus-station, this is a poor area. At night, it is where locals come to see their undercover booze merchant. North of Bab Doukkala, the tatty palm groves have been walled in, who knows to what purpose.

Guéliz, Hivernage and the gardens

*Marrakech médina's other half is the commercial district of Guéliz. The main artery, the **Avenue Mohammed V**, is lined with arcades housing banks, travel agencies and shops for the chic. Though the villas are gradually being demolished, only to be replaced by rusty rose-coloured hotel blocks, Guéliz has a certain charm, especially during the early evening saunter. In the nearby Hivernage to the south, the villas have resisted better, no doubt due to the presence of dignitaries' homes. The hotels are hidden with palm trees aplenty.*

*Further out survive **olive groves** much used by Marrakchis in their leisure moments. As the city has no major parks, the **Jardins de la Menara** and the **Agdal** are places to enjoy greenery away from the traffic-filled streets. Here families stroll and picnic and couples court. At the much-visited Menara, tourists try for the famed photo of the summer pavilion with mountain backdrop, viewed across the still expanses of the reflecting pool.*

*For gardeners, the high point has to be the **Jardin Majorelle**. Here, half-screened by giant bamboo and cactuses, sits the villa- atelier of Jacques Majorelle who made his home and career in Marrakech. Painted an unlikely vivid blue, the villa houses a small craft collection – it's the place to get a feel for quality and pedigree in Moroccan artefacts.*
▸▸ *See Sleeping p110, Eating and drinking p138, Bars and clubs p151*

◉ Sights

Agdal Gardens
Opening hours are unpredictable. Try weekends. Definitely off-limits when the court is in residence. Free. Map 1, H11, p249

The Agdal Gardens, stretching south of the médina, were established in the 12th century under Abd el Moumen and were expanded and reorganized by the Saâdians. The vast expanse, over 400 ha, includes several pools, and extensive areas of olive, orange and pomegranate

Marrakech

59

trees. They are in the main closed when the king is in residence, but are worth a visit on, say, a second trip to Marrakech or if you've got plenty of time. Of the pavilions, the Dar al Baida was used by Sultan Moulay Hassan to house his harem. The largest pool, Sahraj el Hana, is worth a look, although swimming is not advised.

Menara Gardens
0600-0630 daily. Olive groves free, pavilion 15dh. Map 1, H1, p248

From the médina and the Agdal Gardens, Avenue de la Menara leads past the Oliveraie de Bab Jedid to the Menara Gardens. Essentially the Menara Gardens are olive groves, much appreciated by ordinary Marrakchis as a place to stroll and picnic and generally see some green. At the centre of the groves is a rectangular pool with a good view of the Atlas Mountains, as pictured on numerous postcards and brochures. The green-tiled pavilion alongside was built in 1866. Inside, above the small display of carpets and other Amazigh artifacts, is an impressive, painted cedarwood ceiling. Those who know about such things say that the *sahrij* or pool creates its own micro-climate, cooler than the rest of the city when there is a slight summer breeze.

● *There are sometimes* son et lumière *shows here.*

Majorelle Garden
0800-1200 and 1400-1700 in the winter, 0800-1200 and 1500-1900 in the summer. Gardens 20dh, Museum of Islamic Art 15dh. Map 1, A6, p248

The Jardin Majorelle, also called the Bou Saf-Saf Garden, is off Avenue Yacoub al Mansour. This is a small tropical garden laid out in the inter-war period by a French artist, Louis Majorelle, scion of a family of cabinet-makers from Nancy who made their money with innovative art nouveau furniture. Majorelle portrayed the landscapes and people of the Atlas in large, strongly coloured paintings, some of

Menara Gardens

An olive grove surrounds the calm Menara pool. On summer evenings, the temperature is said to be several degrees cooler than the rest of the city.

which were used for early tourism posters. His garden reflects a love for contrast and colour. The buildings are a vivid cobalt blue, the cactuses huge and sculptural. Bulbuls twitter in the bamboo thickets and flit between the Washingtonia palms. The garden now belongs to Yves St Laurent, who also has a house close by. A green-roofed garden pavilion houses a small **Musée d'Art Islamique** with a fine and easily digestible collection of objects.

● *Sensitive souls tempted to try Majorelle Garden blue in decorating schemes back home in northern climes should beware – the result depends on bright sunlight filtered by lush vegetation.*

! In case you need further reason not to eat at the McDonald's on Avenue Mohammed V, be aware that it is considered locally as a potential terrorist target.

The Palmeraie

Free. Beware ferocious dogs if you bike too close to one of the hamlets.
Map 1, A12, p249

Marrakech is surrounded by extensive palm groves. In the original
Prost development plan, no building was to be higher than a palm
tree – and it is illegal to cut down a palm tree – hence the palms
you find growing in the middle of pavements. In recent years the
Palmeraie, a vast area of palms north and east of the city, has
suffered as the property developers have moved in, subdividing
parts of the area for grandiose neo-Oriental villas and the like. So
much for ecological tourism. Nevertheless, the Palmeraie is worth a
look, and is a good place for a drive or a calèche tour. Take the
Route de la Palmeraie, off the P24 to Fès, to explore it. Some bold
souls opt to do the Palmeraie circuit on a bike hired from the
Chemlalia hotels. Be warned, speeding pick up vans and Mercedes
taxis always have priority over cyclists.

High Atlas of Toubkal

Up the Amizmiz road 65 Unusual walking opportunities and working towns.

Up the Taroudant road 66 Austere historic mosque in remote valley, open to non-Muslim visitors, and the Tizi-n-Test pass.

Toubkal National Park 73 Wild mountains centring on North Africa's highest mountain. A region for both committed walkers and day-hikers.

Ourika Valley 76 Day-trippers from Marrakech, skiing at Oukaimeden and a trail-head village.

Telouet (on the Tizi-n-Ticha road) 83 High in the Atlas mountains, a 20th-century warlord's hideaway.

Central Atlantic Coast

Essaouira 86 Morocco's St Malo? Fishing port, picturesque old walls and palm trees, beaches for surfing and camel riding.

Safi and Oualidia 93 An industrious ocean-side town. Busy port next to old médina with working potteries – and ceramic museum and a backwater St Tropez of sorts with oyster restaurants overlooking an Atlantic lagoon.

High Atlas of Toubkal

Up the Amizmiz Road

This involves a trip into a part of the High Atlas less frequented by visitors. You can see a working town on the Haouz Plain at **Tamesloht***, then head for* **Amizmiz***, where there are some good short walks in the foothills behind the village. If you have time, and own car, take the winding mountain road over to* **Ouirgane***, a village with a couple of simple auberge-type hotels on the Taroudant road. With an early start, you could go out from Marrakech via Amizmiz, across to the Taroudant road, lunch at Ouirgane and take in the medieval mosque at* **Tin Mal***.*
▸▸ *See Sleeping p116*

◉ Sights

Tamesloht
Take the main S501 road south out of Marrakech. A few kilometres after the Club royal equestre, the road forks. Go right for Tamesloht and eventually Amizmiz.

Tamesloht, out on the Haouz Plain, 3 km to the west of the S507, was famed as home of the miracle-working man of '366 sciences', one Abdallah ben Hussein El Hassani. Today's visitor finds a ruined kasbah in a typical rural settlement much affected by the droughts of recent years. Richer farmers run water pumps to find water at greater and greater depths. The less fortunate have abandoned their land as simply unprofitable. The tourist attraction? On the main road you'll see shops selling the large terracotta food storage jars now popular for plants in the tasteful houses of Marrakech.

Amizmiz and around
See directions for Tamesloht. There are regular buses (2 hrs, 30 mins), and much quicker grands taxis, to and from Bab Rob in Marrakech.

At the end of the S507, 55 km southwest from Marrakech, Amizmiz has been famed as the home town of acrobats since medieval times. Like many rural settlements, it has a saintly founder, one Sidi Ahmed. As far as sights go, there is a semi-ruined **kasbah** and an important Tuesday morning **souk**. Otherwise, it's a stopping place on the round-the-mountains route to Ouirgane – or a starting point for some **short walks** into the Atlas. The post office, bank and cybercafé are handily located in a new district on the main road as you arrive from Marrakech. Coming in by car, turning off right just after the 'administrative zone', drive up into the foothills to the *maison forestière*. There is some gentle walking along a track above the Assif Anougal, with views down over the villages.

From Amizmiz, there is also a metalled road eastwards to **Ouirgane**. The road runs across rolling open land as far as the Oued Nfis, where there is a ford (*radier* in French on the detailed maps). Then you drive up to the **Tizi-n-Ouzla** (1,090 m) where you get a splendid view of the Assif Amassine valley, with the Toubkal Massif as backdrop. (There's also a **mouflon reserve** signed near the pass.) There then follows a winding descent to the junction with the S501: go right for Ouirgane or left for Asni and Marrakech. **NB** In a wet year, clay from the hillside may crumble onto the upper sections of this Amizmiz to Ouirgane road.

Up the Taroudant road

*Take a drive into the Atlas, up the green Nfis Valley to Ouirgane, where you can stop for lunch, and then carry on to remote **Tin Mal**, cradle of the warrior Almohad dynasty. The restored but unused mosque here is one of the few in Morocco that a non-Muslim may visit.*

▸▸ *See Sleeping p117, Eating and drinking p141*

⊙ Sights

Moulay Brahim

Coming from Marrakech, there is a right turn-off for Moulay Brahim.
The road winding up to the village is narrow so, if driving, take care.
There are plenty of taxis and buses to/from Asni and Marrakech. Taxis
park up below the village. On arrival for a day trip, make sure you ask
what time the last taxis back usually leave.

With plenty of small hotels and eateries, Moulay Brahim is a
popular weekend stop for Red City folk – and worth a quick look if
only to see how Marrakchi families might spend a weekend away.
The village gets particularly busy from June to September, with
people coming to visit the **shrine of Moulay Brahim**, visible
with its green-tiled pyramid roof in the middle of the village. Stalls
selling various scraggy pelts, chameleons and incense indicate that
all sorts of favours may be asked of Moulay Brahim. Indeed, he is
said to be a dab hand at fixing women's fertility problems. (In
Marrakchi culture, its always the women who have such
difficulties.) There is a festive atmosphere, with whole families
coming to rent small semi-furnished apartments. Nicely out of the
way, but still close enough to the big smoke of Marrakech, the
village also has a reputation as a place for illicit liaisons. Out of
season, things are fairly quiet, so the guesthouse accommodation
no doubt has to be kept busy somehow.

Asni

Share taxi from Bab Er Rob or an hour's drive.

After the somewhat nerve-wracking drive through the gorges of
Moulay Brahim, the approach to Asni with its tall stands of cane
and poplar and willow trees comes as something of a relief.
Passing through on a Saturday, you'll find the **souk**, (in a big dusty
enclosure on your left as you come from Marrakech) with its

accompanying chaos of grands taxis, mules and minibuses. In fact, Asni is quite extensive, with houses scattered in clusters along the valley. It makes a good place for a leg-stretch en route to Ouirgane, Tin Mal or Taroudant, or on to the Toubkal National Park – if you can deal with the attentions of itinerant 'Berber' bijou- sellers. The Saturday market has become a tourist attraction but if you are there early it is pleasant to watch the day's events unfold. Watch the locals get an all-over headshave. Or try the open-air dentists if you need a tooth pulled.

Walks and drives around the Plateau du Kik
The best time to visit is spring when the flowers are out.

There is good walking from Asni along the Plateau du Kik to the west of Asni, north to Moulay Brahim and southwest to Ouirgane. The lower slopes are forested while the higher limestone plateau is indicated by a rocky scarp.

Walk up the Tizi-n-Test road to where a mule track goes off right beyond a distinctive conical hill. Continue aiming for the plateau edge. Here there is a choice of going northeast to Moulay Brahim or southwest to Ouirgane. As these are long distances, be prepared to take a taxi back to Asni for the return leg.

For a possible long day walk, starting from Asni, you could take an early local minibus or grand taxi up to **Imlil** (see p73) and then walk downhill through the valley and **Tinifine** (about 8 km from Imlil). After the Assif Imenane joins from the right, cut across to **Tansghart** on the old mule track back into Asni. Total distance around 17 km.

A popular **four-wheel drive day trip** could take you from Marrakech to Asni, up to Moulay Brahim and thence up above the village onto the Plateau du Kik (see local map Amizmiz NH-29XXII-2). From here you may drop down to the villages around **Tiferouine** before heading some 8 km northwest across country to the settlement of **Lalla Takerkoust** and its reservoir lake. Tourist agency trips tend to picnic at encampments near the receding lake shore. The return north to Marrakech is on the S507 Tizi-n-Test road.

Ouirgane

1 hour's drive (61 km) from Marrakech on the valley floor of the Oued Nfis on the S501. The Taroudant bus service from Marrakech stops here, or take a grand taxi from Asni.

Ouirgane is a pleasant village, especially in spring when the almond blossom all around is quite breathtaking. The three hotels (see p117) here have good food and offer the opportunity to explore the valley in easy rambles.

Tin Mal

100 km from Marrakech (about 1 hour 45 minutes' drive, taking things easy), just past the village of Ijoukak. If you are not driving, you can take a Taroudant bus or a grand taxi as far as Ijoukak. Cross the river on the next bridge (often impassable by car), and walk up past Tin Mal village to the mosque. See also walking route to Tin Mal, p76.

High in the Atlas Mountains, on a strategic mule route (now the S501) linking Marrakech and the Haouz with Taroudant, Tin Mal had its hour of glory in the 12th century as holy city of the Almohad Dynasty. For the non-Muslim visitor, the reason for soldiering this far into mountains is the opportunity to see the interior of a major mosque. Built 1153-54 and abandoned not so long afterwards, the building was partly restored in the 1990s.

    To appreciate Tin Mal, rewind back to the early 12th century. In 1122, the pious Ben Toumert, after much roaming in search of Islamic wisdom, returned to Morocco. He created too much trouble in Marrakech with his criticisms of the effete Almoravids. Shortly after, when the mountain tribes had sworn to support him and fight the rulers of the Red City in the name of the doctrines he had taught them, he was proclaimed 'Mahdi', the rightly guided one. In 1125 he established his capital at Tin Mal, then an anonymous sort of hamlet in the heartlands of his tribal supporters. The rough and ready village was replaced with a walled town, soon to become spiritual centre of an empire, a sort of Muslim Lhasa. The first mosque was a simple affair. The building you see today, a low square structure, was the work of Ben Toumert's successor, Abd el Moumen – a student whom the future Mahdi had met in Bejaïa.

From the Taroudant road, looking across to the mosque, you need to imagine it surrounded by a walled town, with banners on the ramparts and smoke rising from the hearths. Tin Mal was the first *ribat*, as the austere Almohad fortresses were called – and subject to a puritan discipline. The Mahdi himself, the most infallible imam, was by all accounts a sober, chaste person, an enemy of luxurious living. All his efforts went into persuading his followers of the truths of Islam – as he conceived them. In fact, his task was not unlike that of the Prophet Mohammed at Medina back in the early days of Islam: how to build a unified community out of a heterogeneous set of competing clans. There was a council of 50 elders to represent the tribes – who cannot have willingly given up their independence.

Standing in the quiet mosque, today mostly open to the sky, looking down the carefully restored perspectives of the arcades, it is difficult to imagine what a hive of religious enthusiasm this place must have been. And after Ben Toumert's death, it was to remain so, as his simple tomb became the focal point for a mausoleum for the Almohad sovereigns.

Tin Mal mosque has a simple exterior. (Perhaps once there was an elaborate minaret.) Unusually, the *mihrab* (prayer niche) is built into the minaret. To the left, as one stands before the *mihrab*, is the

! The prototype for Tin Mal was the Great Mosque at Taza (near Fès), also built by Abd el Moumen. The Koutoubia at Marrakech (Almohad capital as of 1147) was in turn modelled on it.

imam's entrance; to the right is a space for the *minbar*, the preacher's chair, which would have been pulled out for sermons. The decoration is simple: there are several cupolas with restored areas of stalactite plaster work and there are examples of the *darj wa ktaf* and palmette motifs, but little inscription. The technique used, basically plaster applied to brick, is a forerunner of later, larger Almohad decorative schemes.

Essentially, the Tin Mal marks the firm establishment of Ben Toumert's doctrine under his successor, his long-standing follower and companion, Abd el Moumen, who was to lead the Almohad armies into Marrakech. But although the new empire acquired a fine capital well-located on the plain, Tin Mal was to remain its spiritual heart – and a sort of reliable rearbase. It was to Tin Mal that Abd el Moumen sent the treasures of Ben Tachfine the Almoravid.

The tombs of Ben Toumert, Abd el Moumen, Abu Yacoub and Abu Youssef (two further Almohad sovereigns) were at Tin Mal as well, and the place became venerated as a pilgrimage centre, even after the Merinid destruction of 1275-76. The tombs inspired deep respect – and Ben Toumert became a great saint – quite the reverse of what he would have wanted. The Almohad rulers setting off on military adventures would visit Tin Mal to seek success.

Eventually, internal rivalries broke up the clan consensus on which Almohad rule was based. The final act came in the 1270s. The last Almohads took refuge in Tin Mal, led by the vizier Ben Attouch. However, the governor of Marrakech isolated the tiny Almohad group in their mountain retreat, besieged and took the seemingly impenetrable town. The vizier died in battle and the Almohad caliph and his followers were taken prisoner and executed. But the winners went even further. The great Abu Yacoub and Abu Youssef, were pulled from their tombs and decapitated. (The Merinid Sultan is said to have been scandalized.) The Almohads, one-time conquerors of the whole of the Maghreb and much of Spain, were destroyed in their very capital, barely 150 years after they had swept away the Almoravids.

When Tin Mal was studied and surveyed by French art historians in the 1920s, the mosque was in an advanced state of decay. The tombs had long since disappeared and strange cults had taken over in the abandoned sanctuary. Under French rule, the central authorities rejected the Caïd Goundafi's proposal to restore the mosque – fearing perhaps a revival of a long-vanished dynasty. In the early 1990s, the mosque came to the attention of a charitable foundation of the ONA (Omnium nord-africain), Morocco's largest conglomerate. Six million dirhams (about £400,000) was raised up for an ecologically correct restoration with absolutely no ferro-concrete. And so the spiritual heart of a medieval Muslim Empire has survived. The villagers, who for centuries had a decaying basilica-mosque at their disposal, now live next to what might become a major stop on the heritage tourism trail. Or alternatively, the mosque may return to fully-fledged religious use. As it is, it is used for Friday prayers.

Onward to Taroudant via the Tizi-n-Test pass

Buses run between Marrakech and Taroudant via the pass but check that they are marked 'par Tizi-n-Test'. Snowfall often blocks the pass in winter, so check the signs on the exit to Marrakech. On the south side of the range, the S501 joins the main east-west P32 linking Ouarzazate to Taroudant.

The S501 from Marrakech to Taroudant is one of the most spectacular routes in Morocco, winding its way up into the High Atlas to the Tizi-n-Test and then down to Taroudant, 'Marrakech's little sister' on the Sous Plain. Driving has been feasible since 1928 when French engineers completed the transformation of mule track into winding metalled road. From the pass, the views over the Sous to the Anti-Atlas mountains are breathtaking. Although some sections are a bit worrying, particularly when you meet a bus, the drive is recommended, particularly if you tie it in with visits to Asni, Ourigane and Tin Mal.

● *For a tajine-stop on this route, try the cheap restaurant La Belle Vue, about 1 km after the pass on the Taroudant side. Cheap rooms are available too but make sure you have a sleeping bag – it gets cold at 2,100 m altitude.*

Toubkal National Park

The most visited area of the High Atlas, popular with trekkers and day-trippers alike. An insight into the life of the once-isolated Amazigh communities, and an opportunity for short walks or even to climb North Africa's highest mountain, the Jebel Toubkal.
▸▸ *See Sleeping p118, Sports p199*

◉ Sights

Imlil

*Take a share taxi from Bab Rob in MArrakech to Asni, then pick up a rough landrover share taxi to Imlil. If driving, take the first left after leaving Asni. **NB** Parts of the road, which runs along the side of a river valley, are occasionally swept away by flash floods in the late summer. Repairs always follow as this is the key route to the key trail head village for Toubkal.*

The biggest village in the Aït Mizane Valley, Imlil is also a major walkers' base. Treks for Toubkal often start here. In the centre of the village is the car park/taxi area with the stone-built CAF hut at the corner of the road, guides' hut and the *Café du Soleil*. There are numerous small cafés and shops, a good baker and a travel agent. Mules are 'parked' to the south of the village, on the left, before the junction. (There is a concrete route indicator on the right, should you be unsure of your direction.) When you arrive, you may be besieged by lots of underemployed blokes, keen to help you in some way or other. Since everyone knows everyone, none are too persistent.

Climbing Toubkal

As usual when walking in the Atlas, it is best to have a local, Tachelhit-speaking guide. For map information, see p34. For a list of Atlas tour operators, see p32.

There are a number of routes up North Africa's highest peak and Imlil is often the departure point for groups heading for the mountain. The least technical route, which requires a little scrambling from the ex-Neltner Refuge to the summit is used by several thousand visitors each year. Other routes are rather more difficult, and therefore less frequented and consequently more peaceful. The following suggested routes require adequate preparation, good maps and the correct equipment for safe and complete enjoyment. A good guide and mules would remove the strain.

Best time to visit

The best time for walking is after the main snows, at blossom time in the spring. Mules cannot negotiate passes until March/April. For some, summers are too hot and visibility in the heat haze is poor. November-February is too cold and there is too much snow for walking, although frozen ground is often more comfortable than walking on the ever-moving scree. Deep snows and ice present few problems to those with ropes, ice axes, crampons and experience. Without these – stay away in winter.

Imlil to Jebel Toubkal

Imlil is the end of the surfaced road but it is possible to reach **Aremd** (also spelt Aroumd) by car up the rough track. It takes about 45 minutes to walk. *Café Lac d'Ifni* makes a good stop here. **Sidi Chamharouchouch** is another 2 hours 30 minutes' walk, going steadily uphill. It is important to bear right after the *marabout* to find the initially very steep, but later steady slope up to the **ex-Nelter Refuge** (3,207 m). Allow 4 hours 30 minutes from Imlil.

Jebel Toubkal by the South Cwm

This is the usual approach for walkers, a long day's walking and scrambling if you want to go up and come back. The route is clearer on the map than it is on the ground – first observe the route from the rear of the ex-Neltner refuge and the large boulders on the skyline. These are the point to aim for. Leave the refuge and go down to the river. Cross over, and up the other side is the main path to the foot of the first of the many screes. Take the scree path up to the boulders which can be reached in just over an hour. From here there is a choice, the long scree slope to the north of the summit or the shorter, steeper slope to the south of the summit ridge. Either way, allow 3 hours 30 minutes.

The summit

The summit is not in itself attractive, especially if people are making calls from their mobile phones. (Who carried up the pieces of iron for the strange pointed structure on the top?) For a good view of sunrise, bivouac in one of the stone shelters. If there is no heat haze, there are views to Jebels Saghro and Siroua but as Toubkal's summit (4,167 m) is plateau-like, other views are limited. Be prepared for low temperatures. Bitter winds blow three out of four days in the spring and autumn. Allow 2 hours to 2 hours 30 minutes for the descent.

Jebel Toubkal by the North Cwm

A guide and/or a good map is essential for this less congested route. Take the track north from the ex-Neltner Refuge, crossing the river after about 1 km near the small ruined building. Hike up towards the north cwm. The screes move here and the path is not very distinct although the direction is clear enough. The way is up the back of the cwm to the left, to the break in the craggy skyline and a col. The summit then lies to the south along the ridge. It is a long hard climb. Allow at least 4 hours for the ascent.

Jebel Toubkal from Ijoukak

Ijoukak, on the S501, 94 km out from Marrakech on the Taroudant/
Tizi-n-Test route, can be reached by bus – although grand taxi is
more reliable. There are toilets and cafés and rooms may be rented
here. If you take the bus a little further, however, you can walk to
Tin Mal about 5 km off the road, just before the largish settlement
of Mzouzit. You can then do a quiet walk back downstream to
Talat-n-Yacoub and Ijoukak, the track following the contours
above the river most of the way.

Talat-n-Yacoub/Ijoukak can also be used as trail-head villages for
approaching Toubkal from the west. From Ijoukak, you head more
or less east along the Assif Agoundis, with the plateaux of Tajgalt
and Tazaghart to the north. (After the Toubkal climb, the return
route takes you via Tizi Oussem with the same plateaux to the
south.) The route up the Assif Agoundis is a steady climb and the
walk along under the crests (provided the snow line is high
enough) provides good views, and in spring a surprising number of
flowers. The most commonly followed tracks lead eventually to the
ex-Neltner Refuge, allowing keen scree scramblers to reach the
summit of Jebel Toubkal. After the descent, you can continue north
via Sidi Chamharouchouch to Aremd and Imlil. After the section
Imlil to Tizi Oussem, walked on most circuits, the route continues
west over the Tizi-n-Ouarhou to Tizgui (1,930 m) and back to
Ijoukak, passing over the Tizi-n-Iguidi to Aït Zitoun, about 6 km
from the Nfis Valley road. Allow 10-14 days for this demanding
circuit if taking in the Jebel Toubkal summit.

Ourika Valley

*With steep-sided gorges and green, terraced fields along a winding
river, the Ourika Valley is a popular day out from Marrakech (with locals
and tourists alike) and is just 45 minutes' drive from the city. In summer
certain sections of the valley are crowded with campers and day-
trippers happy to be away from the hot, dusty air of the plain. Just*

before Aghbalou, the S513 splits, with a right-hand road taking you up to the 'ski' resort of Oukaïmeden. If you carry on straight ahead you get to the trail-head village of Setti Fatma. With a very early start, it would be possible to visit both Setti Fatma and Oukaïmeden on a long day trip from Marrakech with a good, patient driver. In addition to the tagine stalls and small hotels at Setti Fatma, there are now quite a few eating and sleeping options all along the valley.

▸▸ *See Sleeping p118, Eating and drinking142*

◉ Sights

Aghmat

Take the S513 south from Bab Rob (of the two roads heading for the High Atlas at this gate, the S513 is the one which runs parallel to the walls around the Kasbah neighbourhood and the Agdal gardens). **NB** *You don't want the Tahanoute/Asni road. For Aghmat, turn off left 29 km from Marrakech.*

For enthusiasts of long-gone dynasties Aghmat (spelt Rghmate on some maps), first Almoravid capital of the region, is now a small settlement nestled in verdant olive groves and plant nurseries. There is a domed **mausoleum**, built entirely in the early 1960s on the orders of the late King Hassan II. Modelled on the Almoravid Koubba el Baroudiyine in Marrakech, the building is dedicated to Youssef ben Tachfine, founder of Marrakech in 1062, the mausoleum's ideological message affirming the ruling Alaouite Dynasty's links with the early Muslim past of the region.

After the mausoleum, explore further to find the vaulted foundations of an early **hammam** building, all that remains of the once-magnificent Almoravid town. Near the nurseries you may spot cones of woven cane, a couple of metres high. These are the raw structure of temporary hammams. Covered in adobe, with water heated outside, they can get hot and steamy, and are much appreciated by country folk unable to get to the city hammams.

Dar Caïd Ourika
Further down the S513, take a left turn some 35 km from Marrakech.

The main market town at the foot of this part of the mountains, Dar Caïd Ourika is also referred to as Tnine Ourika ('Monday souk on the Ourika'). On Mondays therefore, things are pretty lively as mountain men pour in to negotiate a sale or a wedding, meet friends and family, listen to the storyteller or have a haircut. Giant tour buses and crowds of foreign visitors add to the colour. There are very few women at the market, an indication of what a gender-separated society this is. If your donkey needs to be reshod or your sickle sharpened for the harvest, this is the place to be. The market aside, Tnine Ourika has few attractions apart from a **zaouia** and a ruined **kasbah**.

● *If you arrive on market day, look out for the mule and donkey park as you cross the bridge over the usually dry river bed.*

If you want to do a round trip instead of heading on up to Setti Fatma, from the market you can continue east along the road to **Aït Ourir**, a major settlement on the Marrakech to Ouarzazate road (see below). Otherwise, from Dar Caïd Ourika to Setti Fatma is about 50 minutes. As you head up into the foothills, the road winds past a large **pottery** on your left. Indeed, the whole road is lined with shops selling terracotta ware – it's amazing that there's much of the foothills left, so much clay must have been mined.

● *After the pottery is a sign for the Camping Amassine, see p120.*

Setti Fatma
Continue up the S513 to reach Setti Fatma – the end of the line.

Setti Fatma must once have been quite pretty but today, the impression is of lots of new, breeze-block housing, complete with satellite dishes, built among the older stone homes. However, the happy sound of the river saves the day, and Setti Fatma could be a good starting/end point for a trek. The town is noted for its annual

Setti Fatma

Carry on up the Ourika to this summer resort for the Marrakech masses.

summer *moussem* (country fair), seven waterfalls and 100-year-old walnut trees. There is also a small weekly **souk**, a useful **bureau des guides de montagne** and quite a wide choice of basic accommodation, as befits a popular summer tripper destination.

The main part of Setti Fatma entails a climb up on the far side of the river to the road. At the main village, cross over to the boulders and grassy area where the youth of Marrakech picnic and relax. There are a number of cheap café-restaurants along the bank, all much of a muchness. The seven **cascades** are a 30-minute scramble up from Setti Fatma, following the path up behind the first café, and there are plenty of young men and kids who will help you find the way. There is a café perched up where the path ends, beside the first waterfall.

Setti Fatma makes a good base for exploring the **Jebel Yagour**, a plateau region famed for its numerous prehistoric **rock carvings**. (About 10 km from Setti Fatma is Tachedirt, where there is a *Refuge du CAF*.) If you don't have much time, it is feasible to do three-day treks up onto the plateau. To set up a trek, contact the *Bureau des guides de montagne*, on your right before the hotels. They have leaflets laying out details of itineraries and prices. By way of example, a three-day trip into the Yagour or the three-day hike from the Ourika Valley to the Toubkal Valley, possible from April to October, costs around 1,000dh per person for 2-3 people, less for larger groups, price includes guide, all meals, mules and cooks and bivouac equipment. Day walks in the region cost between 120dh and 170dh per person, price includes guide, picnic and tea in a local house. Half-day walks up to the fifth cascade cost 50dh per person, less if the group has more than four people.

Oukaïmeden

Access is via the S513 Ourika Valley road – but forking right 43 km out of Marrakech, instead of left for Setti Fatma. There are daily buses from Bab Rob in winter. Determined walkers might want to take the piste from the S501 to the south of Asni and head up into the range.

Oukaïmeden, 'the meeting place of the four winds', is Morocco's premier ski resort – although the ski side of things is a little over-emphasized in the official tourist literature. Snow or no snow, it's a pleasant sort of place, some 2,600 m up in the Atlas and a two-hour drive from Marrakech, making it a fine day trip from the city. In winter you can enjoy the spectacle of Moroccan families having fun in the snow; in summer, a leisurely look at the area's prehistoric rock carvings and possibly a clamber up Jebel Oukaïmeden are in order. In winter hotels and restaurants are open but in summer the resort is less busy with many places closed.

The resort is open for **skiing** from December to March, with a high ski lift up the 3,273 m Jebel Oukaïmeden. The skiing is very variable and good skiable snow is never guaranteed. The hot African sun means that the snow melts during the day only to freeze again at night. However, as soon as there is snow, people flock down from Casablanca with their gear. There are instructors working in the resort, plus a ski shop near the *Hotel de l'Angour*. The ONEP, Morocco's national water board, is responsible for the ski-lifts and is putting in some money to upgrade facilities.

In summer you can **walk**, **climb** and even **parasail**. Also, look out for the **prehistoric carvings** on the rocky outcrop below the dam wall – it takes about 20 minutes to get to them with the right guide. There are further carvings on the flat rocks among the new chalets.

Birders should get some good sightings at Oukaïmeden, including golden eagles (2 m wingspan), the larger lammergeier and some acrobatic flying from smaller booted eagles. Less spectacularly, the resort is home to black redstarts, noisy red-billed choughs, blue rock thrushes and black wheatears. Keep eyes peeled for a glimpse of the magnificent Barbary sheep.

North of Oukaïmeden is **Jebel Tizerag**, 2,784 m, with an easy track almost to the top. It is only 200 m higher than the resort itself, but the views are magnificent.

Tizi-n-Tichka route

Of the two mountain routes over the High Atlas to the southern side of the mountains, the P31 from Marrakech to Ouarzazate, and its Tizi-n-Tichka pass, is the larger road and safer option. Completed in 1936 by the Foreign Legion, the P31 gives stunning views. It runs through the full range of Atlas environments, from the Haouz plains, through the verdant foothills of the Oued Zat, to the barren peaks of the Atlas and the arid regions around Ouarzazate.

▸▸ *See Sleeping p120, Eating and drinking p143*

For the Tizi-n-Tichka route, take the Fès road east out of Marrakech. A right turn takes you onto the P31 Marrakech to Ouarzazate road. Total distance from Marrakech to Ouarzazate is nearly 200 km. You should pace yourself. Good places to stop include upper Taddert (very busy, 86 km from Marrakech), the Tizi-n-Tichka itself which is almost exactly half way, or Ighrem-n-Ouagal, about 118 km from Marrakech where there is an old agadir (granary) to visit. Driving carefully in good conditions, Marrakech to Taddert will take you 2 hours, while Taddert to Ouarzazate is about another 2 hours.

NB Drivers need maximum concentration on this route, especially in the twilight when as likely as not you will meet donkeys and flocks of sheep wandering across the road, guided by small children. Clapped-out local buses break down, and there are some very hairy bits leading up to the pass after Taddert. Don't cut corners. Fossil sellers hanging out at viewpoints and café stops are a further hazard. Also note that in winter, there can be heavy cloud cover, snow storms and icy rain, reducing visibility and making the road extremely slippery. In such conditions, the road is not much fun at night. If snow cuts the pass, then the Gendarmerie royale puts the snow barriers down.

The road to Ouarzazate

At 36 km from Marrakech, you are on the Aït Ourir by-pass. Then the road climbs through the foothills with some splendid views down over the olive groves of the **Oued Zat**. About 46 km from Marrakech, look out for the turn off right (south) to **Larbaa Tighdouine**, a small settlement of concrete houses down in the valley. There's an entertaining minor excursion here: ford the river by mule and ride up to the tiny springs of **Sidi el Ouaji**. Local families fill plastic bottles with the water, reputed for its curative powers. Under the trees around the spring are the usual tea and tajine stands. Walkers note: from Larbaa Tighdouine, you can trek on up to the Plateau du Yagour (with its prehistoric rock carvings) and eventually, over to Setti Fatma (see above).

Back on the P31, climbing fairly steeply, you'll pass the Grouka hunting reserve followed by some Forestry Department buildings, a survival of French times. Shortly before the high pass is the village of **Taddert**, sprawling in two fairly unsightly parts. Take a tagine-break in upper Taddert, the best eaterie being the last one on your right, as you head for Ouarzazate. Shortly after Taddert, a more peaceful café sits conveniently below a hairpin bend before the big climb to the pass itself.

A few kilometres after the pass, and 19.5 km from Taddert, is a sharp turning on the left which takes you onto 20 km of narrow but tarmacked road leading to **Kasbah Telouet** (see below). From the pass the road winds and sweeps down to Ouarzazate. At **Ighrem-n-Ouagal** (1,970 m) there is a fine fortified granary to visit. At **Agouim**, 126 km from Marrakech, a piste comes in from the west. The next point of interest is **Amerzgane**, where there is a turn-off right (west) for Taroudant and the neighbouring ruins of **Tasgedlt**. At 191 km from Marrakech, there's a right turn off onto the road for Zagora which enables you to avoid Ouarzazate – and passes just by the spectacular **Kasbah of Tiffoultoute**.

Telouet

An eagle's nest of a place, high in the mountains, Telouet is something of a legend. It has one of the most spectacular kasbahs in the Atlas, megalomaniac and decaying. The bloodstained history of the dynasty which built it is recounted in Gavin Maxwell's Lords of the Atlas. *Today, Telouet with its flocks of parked four-wheel drive vehicles is for tourists. Within living memory, however, the village's name was synonymous with the repressive rule of the Glaoui brothers. Interesting though Telouet is, it probably comes number three on the excursions from Marrakech list, after Tin Mal and Ouirgane, and Asni/Imlil/Aremd. However, easily accessible, it is still one of the great sites of mountain Morocco and an extraordinary display of quasi-medieval power created in the 20th century. The effect is not dissimilar to mock lairdish castles in the Scottish Highlands.*

» *See Sleeping p120, Eating and drinking p143*

It is possible to do Marrakech to Telouet and back on a very rapid half-day excursion using your own transport. Otherwise, there are slow buses from Bab Aghmat daily at 1500 and 1900, while the Telouet to Marrakech service departs 0700 and 1100. Souk day is Thursday, so there are more taxis on that day. In your own car or, better still, 4WD with an experienced local driver, you will cover much, much more.

Visiting Telouet

As visitors are frequent, the uniformed gardien *is programmed to emerge to the roar of a Toyota 4WD. There is no heritage foundation to look after Telouet – tip the 'warden' 20dh a head after your visit.*

Bloodthirsty and short is the history of Telouet and its kasbah. This is a tale of chance and cunning, of how two brothers of an Atlas tribe, sons of an Ethiopian slave woman, by force of arms and character, came to rule over much of southern Morocco in the early 20th century. As it is a story in which neither of the main players, French and Moroccan, appear in a glorious light, contemporary historians have preferred to leave the main episodes alone. These were turbulent times in Marrakech and the mountains as first the Moroccan monarchy and then the French skirmished with the southern tribal leaders to achieve dominance. The dénouement, which came shortly after Moroccan independence in 1956, was fatal to Glaoui power.

Surprisingly perhaps, there are almost no eyewitness accounts of Telouet at the height of Glaoui power. None of the former inhabitants have written on their home and no doubt the foreign writers and intellectuals of the 1930s were too preoccupied with

! So how was Telouet paid for? Concessions for mining operations across the Glaoui lands apparently produced more than satisfactory returns. In Paris between the two world wars, the Glaoui was synonymous with wealth and excess.

Marrakech to make it up to the mountains. Gavin Maxwell gives a short description of the fortress gripped by winter, just after a great blizzard which left thousands of goats suffocated on the mountainsides. As the snow melted, ravens, crows and kites gorged themselves on the carcasses. At sundown, "the air was dark with them as with a swarm of locusts; they homed for Telouet in their thousands, …till the branches of the trees broke under them, till the battlements of the castle were foul with their excreta".

Abandoned before completion, the Kasbah of Telouet as we see it today is the result of 20th-century building schemes implemented by T'hami, the second great Glaoui chief. Once through the wooden wicket gate, you'll be shown up staircases and along corridors where sand storms have turned the plaster a dusty pink. Entering the **state apartments**, you pass under a photograph of the late Hassan II, kitted out in shades and white hooded robe. (Perhaps the Alaouites always get the last word – Hassan II's father, Mohammed V, was the victim of Glaoui plotting with the French in the early 1950s.) The great reception rooms are still splendid with their cedar ceilings and crumbling stucco, perfect transposition of late 19th-century Moroccan urban taste to the mountains. Imagine a log fire and flunkeys flitting among clubbish leather armchairs.

A visit to Telouet concludes with a clamber up to the **roof**. Keep tight hold of the kids, as there are plenty of unsafe drops and skylights are empty holes where glass should be. Steel T-beams dangle into the emptiness where ceilings have collapsed, fissured adobe walls lean inwards. From these terraces, you can get an idea of the size of 'the labyrinth at whose heart one might expect the minotaur', to quote a visitor during the palace's heyday.

● *Look out for the silk-weave panels above the zelige in the room on your right as you enter the inner 'state' patio.*

Essaouira Harbour
Down the docks in Essaouira, waiting for the catch to come in.

Central Atlantic Coast

Essaouira

*Essaouira, 'little picture', is one of those stage set places: you half
expect to see plumed cavalry coming round the corner, or a camera
crew filming some diva up on the ramparts. A purpose-built 18th-
century military port, it doesn't seem to have changed much since the
end of the days of sail. The port hums with activity, the chunky stone
ramparts stand guard. In town, the walls are white, windows and
shutters a cracked and faded blue, while arches and columns glow a
sandy camel-brown. Three crescent moons on a city gate provide a
touch of the heraldic, while the surfers and the much- exhibited local
naïve school of artists hint at Essaouira's hippy days, back in the
1970s. Tall feathery araucaria trees and palms along the ramparts
add a Mediterranean touch. Only two hours by road from Marrakech,
Essaouira has become popular with day-visitors. And as in the Red*

City, the European gentrifiers have arrived in droves, buying up the picturesque (if damp and crumbling) courtyard houses. Essaouira's annual big moment comes in late May. Temporary stages go up on the parking lot outside the walls, and into the night the town thrills to the thrum of the guembri and Arabo-jazz fusion. Musicians from around the world come in to make this Morocco's most happening musical event.

▸▸ *See Sleeping p120, Eating and drinking p144, Festivals p169*

◉ Sights

The médina

Museum of Sidi Mohammed ben Abdallah, **T** 044-472300. *Officially: 0830-1200 and 1430-1800, except Fri 0830-1130 and 1500-1830, closed Tue. However, renovation works have kept the museum closed. At the time of writing, the re-opening date was uncertain. 10dh.* Galerie des Arts Frédéric Damgaard, **T** 044-784446. *0900-1300 and 1500-1900.* Map 5, p256

Enclosed by walls with five main gates, the médina is Essaouira's major attraction. Entering from Bab Doukkala, the central thoroughfare is **Rue Mohammed Zerktouni**, which leads into Avenue de l'Istiqlal, where there is the **Grand Mosque**, (closed to non-Muslim visitors) and just off, on Derb Laâlouj, the **Ensemble Artisanal** and the **Museum of Sidi Mohammed ben Abdallah**, which houses the Museum of Traditional Art and Heritage of Essaouira, an interesting collection of weapons and handicrafts including woodwork and carpets. A former riad, there are also examples of marquetry-decorated stringed

! Orson Welles used the ramparts of Essaouira – and other sights on Morocco's Atlantic coast, including the great vaulted cisterns at El Jadida – as settings for his film version of Shakespeare's *Othello*.

▶ Precious oil of Essaouira

Approaching Essaouira from Marrakech, the land becomes more rolling as you near the Atlantic. In the stoney fields, you spot an unfamiliar tree – a sort of oversized, dishevelled olive tree. The branches twist and dip, almost to the ground. This is the arganier, producer of the famed argan oil. You may even see a tree-full of goats, browsing on the foliage. (In places, shepherds wait to slow down passing visitors' cars. It's show time. For a small fee, they'll chase their flock up into the branches to pose for a snap.)

The argan is a botanical oddity, the tropical tree that survived north of the Sahara when the jungles died away thousands of years ago. It doesn't need much rain, but likes a warmish climate tempered by ocean mists. Although oil has been made from argan fruit for centuries, it was in the 1990s that the therapeutic values of the oil achieved international renown.

Once harvested, nothing of the argan fruit is wasted. The core or 'almond' is used to make the precious oil. Its shell, once dry, is used as brasero fuel, while the fleshy outside makes good food for goats. Traditionally produced by women for family use, argan oil is now also made by co-operatives, bringing some prosperity to poor villages in Essaouira's hinterland.

Beware cheap imitations mixed with other oils. Argan oil, though more orange than olive oil, should not be red and there shouldn't be any deposits in the bottle. Try also *amlou*, a sort of runny argan oily spread and various body-oils.

instruments and documents on Amazigh music. Upstairs is the ethnographic collection, featuring Chichaoua carpets, embroidery and jewellery. Look out for the mystico-religious signs typical of the area – Essaouira is located at the meeting point of Amazigh

(Tachelhit) and Arabic speaking areas, so such symbols are richer here than elsewhere.

Avenue de l'Istiqlal leads into Avenue Okba ben Nafi, on which is the small **Galerie des Arts Frédéric Damgaard**. This private gallery, run by a long-time Danish resident and amateur of all things Souiri, exhibits the work of local painters, for the most part working in a colourful naïve tradition. At the end of Avenue Okba ben Nafi, the gate on the right leads into **Place Prince Moulay El Hassan**, the heart of the town's social life. The town's souks are mainly near the junction between Rue Mohammed Zerktouni and Rue Mohammed El Gorry, although there is an area of woodworkers inside the **Skala** walls to the north of Place Prince Moulay El Hassan, where fine pieces can be picked up after some bargaining banter.

At the northeast end of Rue Mohammed Zerktouni, close to Bab Doukkala, is the **mellah**, the former Jewish quarter, an area of significant size, underlining the prominence of the Hebrew population probably present in Essaouira at the time of its foundation. As in other North African cities, the Jews at one time formed an important minority but they deserted their homes in the 1950s and 1960s. Today the mellah is the poorest quarter of the town (most houses lack running water and loos). There are rumours, however, of a major hotel project. Many houses have ocean views, so the site is obviously attractive to would-be developers.

The Harbour and Skala
Entry to Skala du Port is via a kiosk close to the Porte de la Marine. 10dh. Map 5, D2, p256

Off Place Prince Moulay El Hassan is the small but vibrant harbour, which principally supports a fishing fleet, and is worth a visit. It is still possible to see the work of traditional shipbuilders and

! The term *mellah* (Arabic for salt) goes back to Fès, where the
• Jewish *houma* (quarter) was located close to a salty spring.

repairers on the bustling quayside and nearby the lively fish market and open-air restaurant stalls serve many varieties of grilled fish (typically prices range from 10-25dh). The stone sea gate (the **Porte de la Marine**) linking harbour and médina was built in 1769 under Sultan Sidi Mohammed ben Abdallah. Local legend runs that the designs were by an Englishman converted to Islam. The neo-classical pediment displays the year of construction (1184 of the Hegira). From the Porte de la Marine you can head round the harbour to the **Skala du Port**, an old Portuguese sea defence and battery. From the top of the bastion there are extensive panoramic views of the harbour and the offshore islands, the **Iles Purpuraires**. The term 'skala', meaning coastal fortification in Moroccan Arabic, derives from the French 'escale' (landing point).

Skala de la Ville
Free. Map 5, C2, p256

Further to the north of Place Prince Moulay El Hassan it is possible to get on to the ramparts of the Skala de la Ville from Rue de la Skala, close to its junction with Rue Darb Laâlouj. Crenellated walls protect a 200-m long raised artillery platform and an impressive array of decorated Spanish and other European cannon. From the tower of the North Bastion there are fine views north along the sea wall to the mellah and over the médina with its white buildings and blue shutters. The woodworkers' souks are also here in arched chambers underneath the ramparts.

The Church
Quartier des Dunes, behind the Hotel Sofitel. For details of services, contact the presbytery on **T** 044-475895. *Free. Map 5, F4, p256*

Like other historic Moroccan coastal cities – Tangiers, for example, Essaouira has a long tradition of religious cohabitation. With the influx of foreign residents and visitors, the church has experienced something of a revival. During the spring **Festival des Alizés**, see p169, concerts are occasionally held here, too. While not of any great architectural interest (ecclesiastical architecture buffs should find time to take a look at the Neo-Moorish St Andrews, Tangiers or the cathedrals in Casablanca and Rabat), Essaouira's church is the only one in Morocco which is allowed to ring its bells on Sunday for Mass at 1000.

Cemeteries
Free, but the warden on hand to let you in welcomes a contribution – say 10dh a head. Best visited in mornings. Map 5, A6/7, p256

Outside the northern walls of Essaouira, just outside Bab Doukkala, are the Christian and Jewish cemeteries. The entrance to the **Christian Cemetery** is in the wall where the horse-drawn carriages park up, on your left as you come out of town through Bab Doukkala. Here you'll find the graves of various European consuls who died converting Mogador into a trading post. About 200 m further on is the entrance to the **Jewish Cemetery**. If you can find the man with the key (knock loudly), you may discover the resting place of Leslie Hore-Belisha, inventor of the first pedestrian crossing light.

Beaches
The P8 which runs from the south into Essaouira takes you to Diabat.

Broad stretches of windy sand make Essaouira a surf location – although such beaches are fine for walking, too. The trade wind (know locally as the *alizé*) makes it cold for swimming, but ideal for surfing. The northern **Plage de Safi** is fine in the summer, but can

!
•
The ruins of Borj el Baroud inspired the Jimmy Hendrix song, *Castles in the Sand*. For hippies, Essaouira smoked with inspiration ... thrumming guembris, mystic rituals, white walls awaiting the flower-power painters' touch.

be dangerous during windy weather. South of the town, the beach is great for football – surely Essaouira must be a school for soccer champions. Past the Oued Ksob, the waves break against the remains of **Borj El Baroud**, a Portuguese fort. Local legend runs that this Lusitanian outpost was swallowed by the sand. A Soussi magician put the hex on it, as his region's trade was being ruined by the Portuguese. The **mouth of the Ksob** is popular with birders, who point their binoculars at a large colony of yellow-legged herring gulls and a variety of migrating seabirds including black, little, sandwich, whiskered and white-winged terns. After the oued, you reach the village of **Diabat**, once famed as a hippy hangout. The *Auberge Tangaro*, one of the region's legendary small hotels, survives from this time. Below Diabat, incoming tides turn the Oued Ksob into an impassable river.

Iles Purpuraires

These islands, visible from Essaouira, are strictly off limits to avoid disturbance of the birds. In calm weather, boat trips from the fishing port may run close to the islands. Your riad or hotel (or the port) may carry information.

Ocean mists give the inaccessible Purpurine Islands an extra mystery. In good weather the isles and their most famous residents, the rare Eleonora's falcons, are visible with a good telescope from the jetty in Essaouira port. (Another area frequented by the falcons is the mouth of Oued Ksob to the south of the town, see above.) The creation of a regular daily ferry service to the islands is hopefully only a rumour: nothing should be allowed to disturb the nesting Eleonora's falcons – after all they are threatened with extinction and have flown all the way from Madagascar. The falcons are onto a good thing on the Purpurines: the hundreds of gull nests provide ready fodder.

The islands' name comes from the purple dye made there from molluscs in Phoenician and Roman times and on the main island, l'île du Pharaon, archaeologists in the 1950s found remains of vats for making *garum*, that fishpaste delicacy essential to Roman banquets. All in all, it is evident that the Purpurine Islands were quite the ancient off-shore industrial zone, producing luxury items for the Mediterranean élite.

Safi and Oualidia

*Sprawling and industrial, Atlantic Safi has a small médina and a lively fishing port. Its walls testify to a past devoted to keeping European marauders out of Morocco. Despite its renown as a centre for fine, traditional pottery, Safi is probably best left to enthusiasts – although some will find a gritty charm here. For those in search of architectural oddities, the **médina** contains a fragment of a cathedral in the Manueline Gothic style – all that the Portuguese had the time to build during their brief occupation in the 16th century. Unlike El Jadida to the north, where they clung on into the 18th century, Safi was a Portuguese fortified enclave for a mere 33 years.*

Once capital of the Abda region, Safi today is a town with a sense of cosmopolitan identity lost since independence and the arrival of rural migrants. Many Safiots were active in the nationalist movement, and there is something of a Safi lobby at government level, pushing to get the all-powerful phosphate industry – the biggest regional employer – to clean up its act. Getting the municipal rubbish collection services operational would be a start, locals are heard to grumble.

*North of Safi, almost halfway to El Jadida, **Oualidia** is altogether more restful and bijou. Named for the Saâdian Sultan El Oualid, builder of a kasbah here in the 1630s, the town is now famed for its oyster farms – and the restaurants for consuming aforesaid slippery morsels. There is a small fishing port, a lagoon, safe swimming and ample amusement for twitchers, as the inlets and beaches are much appreciated by migrating birds in autumn and spring. Busy in summer, Oualidia is more than tranquil for the rest of the year.*

▶ *See Sleeping p124, Eating and drinking p146*

Grands taxis and buses run from Marrakech and Essaouira to Safi, and from Safi to Oualidia. Grand taxi departures from Marrakech to Oualidia are few. Check with the CTM in Marrakech whether the bus service to Safi has been resumed. From Marrakech, both grands taxis and buses leave for Safi from the Bab Doukkala public transport hub. Journey time for Safi should be under two hours by grand taxi, longer for private-line bus. For Oualidia, the time is likely to be closer to four hours, depending on vintage of bus. Best option: early departure from RAK by grand taxi. Safi can also be reached by rail: change at Benguerir for the twice-daily branch line service off the main RAK to Casablanca line.

⊙ Sights

Safi médina
Best visited as a short half-hour ramble in the morning, when stalls are at their liveliest. National Ceramics Museum, **T** 044-463895. *0830-1200 and 1400-1800. 10dh.*

The médina, with its ramparts and large towers, slopes westwards towards the sea and can be entered by the main gate, **Bab Chaâba**. The main thoroughfare which runs from Place de l'Indépendence to Bab Chaâba is **Rue du Socco**, around which are the main souks. It is a busy, bustling area, with shops and street stalls selling all manner of food, jewellery, cheap toys and plastic goods. Close to the northern wall of the médina near Bab Chaâba is the pottery souk (see The Potters' Quarters page 96), crammed with locally made pots and plates. This leads on up some steps to an open courtyard with attractive archways housing further pottery stalls. Just off the Rue du Socco is the **Grand Mosque** (off limits to non-Muslims) and behind it the minimal ruins of a Gothic church built by the Portuguese, originally intended as part of a larger cathedral. (For the record, these are the only surviving remains of a Gothic building in Africa.)

Dominating the east flank of the médina is the **Kechla**, (lit. barracks), all towers and green-tiled roofs. Built by the Saâdians and later extended, it shelters the charming Riad el Bahia, now home to the **National Ceramics Museum** (Musée national de la céramique). From here you have outstanding views over the médina and the potters' quarter at Bab Chaâba. The entrance opens out into the main courtyard, gardens and a terrace. Displays of ceramics are divided into three sections: historic, local, and contemporary. Look out for the fine 20th-century Safi artistic pottery.

Dar el Bahar

Entry is under an archway, inscribed 'Château de Mer', opposite the Hotel Majestic. 0830-1200 and 1430-1800. 10dh.

Just outside the médina ramparts, overlooking the sea, is the Dar el Bahar (Sea Tower), governor's residence and prison, built by the Portuguese in 1523. In the late 14th century, the site was occupied by a fortified trading post, used as a base by the Portuguese for their surprise attack on Safi in 1508 that ultimately led to their occupation of the town. The building was restored in the 1960s. Take a quick look, if only for the ocean view. Just to the left of the pay kiosk is a hammam and to the right is the prison tower. Climb the spiral staircase (narrow and dark in places) for the views of the médina, Kechla and port from the top. After returning to the foot of the tower, access to the ramparts on the seaward side of the fortress is via a ramp. Here can be seen an array of Dutch and Spanish cannon pointing out to sea; the cast-marks on two of these show 'Rotterdam 1619' and two others are marked 'Hague 1621', witness to the 17th-century Dutch Republic's role as arms supplier to the Saâdian sultans. The curly Arabic markings are the *tughras* (seals) of the aforesaid sultans.

● *From the top of the southwest bastion, gaze southwards down the coast towards Essaouira.*

The Potters' Quarter, Bab Chaâba

Best visited in the mornings when the workshops are more active. No entrance fee, but lots of temptations to purchase. Note that the best place to buy is not always the stalls below potters' hill. Try the pottery souk in the médina, off Rue du Socco.

A wander through the working potteries of Bab Chaâba is a must in Safi. Children will be particularly fascinated, as they can see all the stages of the pot-making process in and around the tiny workshops. From the port side of the old town, you can cut straight through to the neighbourhood which centres on a shrine to the potters' patron saint, **Sidi Abderrahman**, Moula El Bibane, 'Protector of the city gates'. The whole area became a historic listed neighbourhood in 1920. Safi once produced pottery with an international reputation (and also continues to make the green tiles used on many public buildings throughout Morocco). The recent development of the potteries is an interesting story, shedding light on French policy towards traditional crafts in Morocco.

Today's Safiot potter works much as his early 20th-century ancestor did. Equipment is simple: potter's wheel, basin, reed, pot-shard and a few planks to leave pots drying in the shade. The clay comes in the form of large chunks which need breaking up and softening in water. On the second day of preparation, the clay is left in the sun before being kneaded by feet in big round pats on a bed of ashes. After a secondary hand-kneading to remove stones, the clay is ready. In dark workshops, well out of the bright daylight, the potters can be seen hard at work at their foot-operated wheels.

Painting and glazing were areas in which numerous experiments were conducted under Algerian master potter Boujemaâ Lamali in the 1920s and 30s. Before painting, the pot has to be dipped in a mixture of white clay and water, to cover the original clay colour. (Traditionally, the glaze – a liquid composed of tin, lead and silicate – was applied before coloured designs.) Generally five colours are used: white, blue, green, yellow and brown. (Lamali revived the old colours of Safi pottery, which had disappeared with the ease of producing Fassi blue and white designs.) The motifs are painted in outline by the *maâlem*, and the apprentice does the colouring in.

The pot-painters, often women, are highly skilled workers. The pots are carefully piled in the kilns before re-firing. A small tripod or *chouka* is used to separate the bigger pieces so that air can circulate in the kiln. The three marks left after this second firing are painted in afterwards. The motifs have names like honeycomb, scorpion, butterfly wing, olive kernel and bull's eye but many of the designs today are rather garish.

Profits for the workshop owners are potentially very good. The clay brought in from quarries some 5 km outside Safi costs a mere 200dh per lorry load. Skilled potters operate on a piece work basis, making between 500dh to 600dh a month. The guys who do the carrying, clay-kneading and kiln-stoking obviously make less. This could be the place to design and order your own dinner service.

Beaches near Safi
Sidi Bouzid, bus route 15.

The best local beach is **Sidi Bouzid**, just north of the town, with cafés and the *Le Refuge* seafood restaurant. Further afield is the **Lalla Fatma** beach, just past Cap Safi. Locals with own transport go further afield to **Plage Souiriya**, some 30 km to the south.

Youssoufia
15km off the P12 Safi to Marrakech road.

If making a day trip to Safi by car, it's worth making a side trip to Youssoufia, named for Moulay Youssef, great-grandfather of the present king. Youssoufia is the source of the phosphates shipped out through Safi. The town was formerly named **Louis-Gentil**, after the French mining engineer who discovered the phosphate deposits. On a wooded hill above the town is the strange sight of pitched-roof villas in a French-style garden suburb. Here colonial mine management once lived in considerable comfort.

Oualidia

Oualidia sits above a peaceful lagoon, kept topped up with ocean water by two breaches in a natural breakwater. Above the beach, the skyline on the wooded hillside is dominated by the **kasbah** built in 1634 by Saâdian Sultan El Oualid (a track to the right off the S121 opposite the turning to Tnine Gharbia leads up to the building) to defend the potentially useful harbour. Below it is the now disused **royal villa** built by the present king's grandfather, Mohammed V, as a summer palace. The lagoon and beach provide an ideal sheltered location for sailing, surfing, windsurfing and fishing, and riding may be a possibility too. From late June to September, Oualidia is very busy. The beach gets very crowded and the water is none too clean. Off-season, you have the beautiful surroundings almost to yourself, spiced with local colour on Saturday, market day. Oualidia's big claims to fame are oysters and tomatoes. Beds producing the aphrodisiac mollusc came into production in the late 1950s. Annual production is around 200 tonnes, consumed mainly in Morocco. The tomato and other early vegetables are farmed under plastic for local and European consumption.

For a change of beach, head for **Lalla Fatna**, just 2 km outside the main village. For those with a car, the **Kasbah Gharbia** about 20 km to the southeast on the S1336 is a possible side-excursion. The kasbah is a huge enclosure, with a large white building in the centre, no doubt the home of a local notable in Protectorate times. The locals will be pleased to have visitors, and will no doubt show you round.

▸▸ *See Sleeping p125, Eating and drinking p147*

Marrakech hotels range from Spartan places in the médina to the discreet luxury of a restored palace. The latter, often run by their owners, are far more than a place to put your head down for the night. They'll give you a very personal vision of the city's life, albeit through Orientalist spectacles. Since the mid-1990s, riads, as these guesthouses are called, have become central to tourism in Marrakech. Back in the 1960s such palaces, then in full decay, provided havens for millionaires on the run, lured by kif, colour and an oasis sensuality. Carefully balancing luxury and simplicity, the better riads will pamper, at a price, to your every whim. In the nearby Palmeraie, there are villas for the über-rich where the cost of a night's stay is beyond most people's understanding.

In Essaouira, prices in guest houses are lower. Here and in certain areas of the High Atlas – the village of Ouirgane, for example – are some interesting rural retreats. Still in the mountains, walkers will find rough hotels in trailhead villages and local houses where you bunk down for 50dh. The very cheapest night in the Red City, excluding the youth hostel, will be around 80dh.

→ **Sleeping codes**

Price				
AL	2,500dh and above	D	260dh-360dh
A	1,000-2,500dh	E	180-260dh
B	800-1,000dh	F	120-180dh
C	360-800dh	G	60-120dh

Prices are for a double room in high season

Upmarket **guest house** (riad) accommodation is generally in the médina (**Bab Doukkala**, **Bab Leksour** and **Mouassine** north of the Jemaâ el Fna, and off **Riad Zitoun el Kedim**, south of the Jemaâ el Fna) and the **Palmeraie**. There are a small number of agencies proposing riad accommodation (see listings below) as well as those of owner-run riads. Dazzling though guest houses often look on glossy paper, you need to be aware of the potential disadvantages. Is there any heating? What sort of fans are available if there's no air conditioning? What about kids' safety? Is there a mosque nearby? (You may be awoken by the loudspeaker calling people to prayer at 0430.) Riad websites often depict just the master suite – other rooms may be cramped and dark.

Marrakech's big expensive **chain hotels** have spacious public areas, gardens, comfy bars and pools (check if heated in winter). The Méridien Nfis, the Sheraton, the Impérial Borj and the recent Sofitel, are all reliable. Accommodation in the 400-800dh bracket is more problematic. The **medium price hotels**, located in Guéliz, along or off Avenue Mohammed V and Avenue Zerktouni tend to have pokey rooms, indifferent service and traffic noise. (Although a plus point is the handiness of a variety of restaurants and services.)

You'll find **small budget hotels** close to Jemaâ el Fna, in the alleys off pedestrian street Bab Agnaou, off Riad Zitoun el Kedim and in the Kennaria neighbourhood behind the Café-Hotel de France. These hotels fill up early – always try to reserve, especially at peak times of year and during Moroccan public holidays.

Riad rental agencies

The advantage of renting via an agency is that there should be a guaranteed minimum level of service. Properties available are in all sectors of the médina and all agencies have contacts with riad owners in other cities should you wish to spend time on the Atlantic coast or elsewhere in Morocco. Note that prices are as much as 20% higher at peak times of year. Riads with accommodation let directly by the owners are listed in the appropriate areas of the médina.

Marrakech-Médina, Sarl, 102 Rue Dar el Pacha, **T** 044-442448, www.marrakech-medina.com. The oldest of the three main agencies, but said to be past its prime. Riads are classified by palm tree, four palmiers being the most luxurious. The **A/B Dar Kawa** is the most sophisticated, styled in minimalist greys and creams. The **C Riad Lazrak** with 10 rooms and shared loos and showers would suite a large group of close friends.

Marrakech Riads, Dar Chérifa, 8 Derb Chorfa-Lekbir, **T** 044-426430, www.marrakech-riads.net. Established by Abelatif Aït ben Abdallah, a local with years of experience in saving decaying historic property, Marrakech Riads is probably the best of the three agencies. Star property is the grand **A Riad Zellige**, with four doubles. Also popular is the more homely **B/C Dar Sara**.

Riads au Maroc, 1 Rue Mahjoub Rmiza, Cité Lumumba, Guéliz, **T** 044-431900, www.riadomaroc.com. Established in 2000, this agency has a young, dynamic staff. Star properties include the spacious **B Riad Laïla**, not far from Bab Doukkala, complete with small pool in the middle of a jungly patio set with orange trees, two suites and small rooms on the *douirya* or service patio. The website will show you properties for rent across Morocco.

Jemaâ el Fna and around

AL Villa des Orangers, 6 Rue Sidi-Mimoune, **T** 044-384638, villadesorangers.com. *(1) Map 3, G4, p252* Near the new Royal Palace, the Orangers is an exceptional small hotel with three rooms and 13 suites, eight of which have their own terraces. Decor in elegant beiges and woody tones harmonizes with the stucco and carved cedar woodwork. **NB** Closed late July to mid-August.

AL Hotel La Mamounia, Av Bab Jedid, **T** 044-448981, www.mamounia.com. *(2) Map 3, F1, p252* Built in the late 1920s and for years the most luxurious hotel in Morocco, La Mamounia retains its legendary aura. The suite said to have been occupied by Sir Winston Churchill in his retirement is religiously preserved. Prices are sky-high. The extension of the 1980s increased the number of rooms but did little for the hotel's charm. Prefer a smaller, more personable place.

AL Riad El Cadi, 59 Derb El Cadi, Azbezt, **F** 044-378478, (make initial contact via fax or mail). *(3) Map 3, C9, p253* Just off Derb Debbachi, one of the finest riads in Marrakech, developed by a high-ranking German diplomat in his retirement. There are 12 suites and five patios, including one with plunge pool. (The owner, a popular Marrakech figure, recently died and it is to be hoped that the address will continue to function to its original high standards.)

AL Riad Enija, 9 Derb Mesfioui, Rahba Kedima, **T** 044-440926, riadenija@cybernet.net.ma. *(4) Map 3, B8, p253* Two spacious neighbouring riads restored by a Scandinavian décoratrice. A more imaginative (some would say delirious) interpretation of Occident meets Orient would be hard to find. Jungliferous central courtyard, and every suite has a bijou name. Worth a short stay if you have the funds.

A Dar el Assad, 29 Derb el Hajra, Derb Debbachi, **T** 044-427065, 06-1130820. *(5) Map 3, C/D9, p253* Owner Daniel Bainvel, once an antiques dealer in Nantes, has given this riad an incomparable Second Empire meets the Ottomans style. Four en suite rooms and more likely to be added. There's a small patio filled with luxuriant vegetation, a copious breakfast and a wonderful roof terrace. The downside? You may have to stay two nights minimum at peak times.

A La Maison Bahira, 54 Rue des Banques, Kennaria, **T** 044-426609, information and reservations with Marion Théard on **T** 06-1757176, see also www.bahira.com. *(6) Map 3, C8, p253* A rare find: a small, simply-furnished courtyard house just off Jemaâ el Fna, down a passage scented with a fig tree, opposite the Hotel Kennaria. No chichi decoration here – all is calming whites and deep blue woodwork. Can sleep up to six. Prices start at €200 for the whole house for two. A fantastic base for a quiet week.

B Jardins de la Koutoubia, 26 Rue de la Koutoubia, **T** 044-388800, hotel.jardinskoutoubia@iam.net.ma. *(7) Map 3, D5, p252* An efficiently-run *faux riad* on the site of one of Marrakech's finest palaces, the sadly demolished Dar Louarzazi. Rooms, which open onto galleries running round the central pool courtyard, are on the small side. Good as a fall back if your preferred riad is full. Its plus points are ease of access, the best pool this close to 'la Place' and the nearly poolside piano-bar, one of only a handful in the médina.

B/C Riad el Borj, 63 Derb Moulay Abd el Kader, Derb Debbachi, **T** 044-391223, manager on **T** 06-5248302, 06-1675942, www.ryadelborj.com. *(8) Map 3, C9, p253* One of the simpler riads, 5 mins east from Jemaâ el Fna down Derb Debbachi. Friendly, well run – could suit a family for a couple of nights (nothing too bijou or breakable). Rooms are themed: ask for the Ouarzazate room up on the second floor (600dh a night).

D Hotel Gallia, 30 Rue de la Recette, **T** 044-445913. *(9) Map 3, E6, p252* Clean, conveniently located. Head down Rue Bab Agnaou from Jemaâ el Fna; the Gallia is at the end of a narrow street on the left. A 1930s building with beautifully planted courtyard. Had a rather sulphurous reputation but is now very smart. Good value for money, so reserve well in advance. The ancestor of the riad guesthouses, plenty of hot water, a few rooms with air conditioning. Some rooms dark, so ask to inspect them if they aren't full.

D Grand-Hotel Tazi, Rue Bab Agnaou, **T** 044-442787. *(10) Map 3, F6, p252* At the far end of pedestrian Rue Bab Agnaou from Jemaâ el Fna. Breakfast 20dh extra. Memorable rooms with extravagantly- painted ceilings and furniture. The bar, one of the only ones in the médina, is open to non residents. There's a licensed Moroccan restaurant, too. Convenient for sights and services, but perhaps a tad overpriced.

E Hotel de Foucauld, Av el Mouahidine, **T** 044-445499. *(11) Map 3, E5, p252* A good hotel (same management as *Tazi*), 33 rooms, restaurant and bar. Easily located just opposite the well-planted square de Foucauld, aka Arset el Bilk. Used by trekking groups.

E/F Hotel Ali, Rue Moulay Ismaïl, **T** 044-444979. *(12) Map 3, E6, p252* Especially recommended for those intending to go climbing/ trekking in the Jebel Toubkal region as the guides are here. Mixed reports on its cleanliness, but it's friendly and has good, cheapish Moroccan food. Also has internet facilities, and sells trek-maps of mountain areas at 160dh a sheet. Twinned with the Hotel Farouk in Guéliz.

D Hotel Fantasia, 184 Arset El Maâch, **T** 044-426545. *(13) Map 3, F6, p252* The Marrakech hotel closest to the Oriental house of the three little pigs. The tiling truly hurts the eyes. That said, the 35 en suite rooms are clean and comfortable, the roof terraces extensive.

F **Hotel Central Palace** , **T** 044-440235. *(14) Map 3, E6, p252* Well signed in an alley off Rue Bab Agnaou, on your left as you come from Jemaâ el Fna. 40 rooms, 120dh for a twin room. One of the best cheapies. Also has an annexe for housing overflow. Top floor rooms very hot in summer – you may wind up sleeping on the roof. Recommended but make sure you reserve well in advance.

F **Hotel Icbhilia**, on a street linking Rue Beni Marine and Rue Bab Agnaou (turn left off the latter just before Cinéma Mabrouka), **T** 044-390486. *(15) Map 3, E6, p252* The street-facing rooms are noisy but it's fine for a night or two. Cyber-café in basement of building.

F **Hotel CTM**, on Jemaâ el Fna, in the corner near the start of Riad Zitoun el Kedim, **T** 044-442325. *(16) Map 3, D7, p253* Good rooms, some with a view of the square (noisy), often full. Pleasant terrace with a popular café. However, it's not as clean as it could be. **NB** *CTM* buses now go from Av Zerktouni near the Cinéma Colisée in Guéliz.

F **Hotel Souria**, 17 Rue de la Recette, near the Hotel Gallia, **T** 044-426757. *(17) Map 3, E6, p252* One of the smallest hotels in Marrakech. Minute patio filled with pot plants. Nine rooms and bathroom upstairs. Minimalist and tranquil, if a little spartan.

G **Hotel Mimosa**, Rue des Banques, the pedestrian street to the side of the *Café de France*, **T** 044-426385. *(18) Map 3, D8, p253* Built in 1997 (with tiles everywhere) this place has 16 rooms with washbasins and a cupboard. The shower's free, and there's a decent terrace. Fine for a couple of nights. (1 person 50dh, 2 people 80dh, 3 people 120dh.)

North of Jemaâ el Fna

A **Riad Zellige**, 46 Ihihane, Sidi ben Slimane, **T** 044-426463, www.marrakech-riads.net. *(19) Map 2, D6, p250* 'The House of

Mosaics' is the flagship riad of the city's second riad rental agency, Marrakech-Riads, managed since its beginnings in the late 1990s by the enthusiastic Abdellatif Aït ben Abdallah. (Make time to visit Dar Chérifa, the agency's HQ in Mouassine, see p102.) The principle behind the makeover, established by Quentin Wilbaux, the city's number one riad-restorer, is careful restoration with a few concessions to modern day comforts. One the plus side, it's authentic with no painful Mali-meets-Morocco frills. However, it's a good 30-min trek from 'la Place', up beyond Sidi ben Slimane. But then the médina is a city made for walking. Consult the website for simpler properties managed by Marrakech-Riads, including the pleasant Dar Sara at Bab Doukkala.

A La Maison Arabe, 1 Derb Essehbe, Bab Doukkala, **T** 044- 387010, www.lamaisonarabe.com. *(20) Map 2, H3, p250* Originally a French-run restaurant back in pre-Independence days, 'the Arab house' merits a mention for its status as senior Marrakchi guest house. The building, of little architectural interest, was refurbished by an Italian princeling in the mid-1990s to function as a boutique-ish hotel. Rooms are comfortable if on the small side for the price. Pluses include the out- of-town pool, served by shuttle bus, and the restaurant. Check if the cookery courses are still on offer.

A Riad 72, 72 Derb Arset Aouzal, Bab Doukkala, **T** 044-387629, www.riad72.com. *(21) Map 3, A4, p252* One of the most photographed riads, all chocolate brown and cream textiles and tadelakt, plus minimalist fashionista touches. Stylish. Worth a long stay if you get the vast main suite. Other three rooms a little on the small side for the price. Other features: small garden courtyard, fantastic roof terraces and dinky in-house hammam.

B Tchaikana, 25 Derb el Ferrane, Kaât Benhadid, **T** 044-385150, www.tchaikana.com. *(22) Map 3, A10, p253* The name means 'tea-house' in central Asia, a little curiously perhaps for an impeccable guesthouse a few minutes' walk from the Medersa Ben Youssef. The management is young, enthusiastic and Belgian, the four rooms are grandiose, the styling gives an Afro-minimalist take to the typical Marrakchi riad spaces. Generous breakfasts and meals in the room cooked to order. TV room for kids, central heating and air conditioning. It's a bit too far into the labyrinth for some – but that said, it's very handy for souks and northern médina monuments. Hard to fault. Suite at 1,400dh, room at 900dh.

B Riad Zina, 38 Derb Essabane, Riad Larousse, **T** 044-385242, www.riadzina.ma. *(23) Map 2, G7, p251* Handily located just a few mins' walk off 'la Place', la Zina offers yet another trendy take on the riad refurbishment theme. Main features? Large cactus-planted courtyard, vibrant oranges and ochres. The big draw is the main suite (1,100dh) with its separate salon. It also has spacious roof terraces and it's handy for restaurants *Dar Marjana* and *Dar Moha*, and the Ben Youssef neighbourhood sites.

B/C Dar Mouassine, 148 Derb Snane, just a couple of mins' walk from the Mouassine Mosque, **T** 044-445287. *(24) Map 3, B6, p252* Beautiful patio, tiny pool, video and charming, simply decorated rooms. Pleasant roof terraces, too. Meals to order for around 180dh. One of the best cheaper riads. (Rooms start at 800dh in summer.) Welcome may be a little off-hand sometimes but still a good address at this price in a central neighbourhood.

South of Jemaâ el Fna

AL Les Jardins de la Médina, 21 Derb Chtouka, **T** 044-381851, www.lesjardinsdelamedina.com. *(25) Map 1, H9, p249* Accommodation includes 31 rooms and 5 suites around garden patios. Down in the Kasbah neighbourhood, a southern outpost of 'riad culture' which got off to a good start in 2001. A large scale version of the traditional house, it has charm but not the stifling

Absolutely Fabulousness of so many riads. Restaurants serving Moroccan and Mediterranean (or even Thai) food. The service is efficient, there's a pool (and hammam), and a room for disabled visitors, as well as all the usual features of a good hotel. On the minus side, you'll be taking taxis as Derb Chtouka is a good 25-min hike from Jemaâ el Fna.

A Riad Zinoun, 31 Derb Ben Amrane, Riad Zitoun el Kedim, **T** 044-426793. *(26) Map 3, E7, p253* See p247.

A/B Riad Kaïss, 65 Derb Jedid, Riad Zitoun el Kedim, **T** 044-440141, www.riadkaiss.com. *(27) Map 3, G8, p253* A fine house dating from the 1860s restored by a French architect and aesthete. Around two garden patios, the conversion has found space for eight homely rooms with air conditioning, heating, fireplaces. Some rooms even have private terraces. Highly recommended but very popular. Also a hammam and outdoor plunge pool.

C Hotel Jnane Mogador, 116 Riad Zitoun Kedim, **T** 044-426323, www.jnanemogador.com. *(28) Map 3, E7, p253* New in 2002, 17 rooms with shower/WC, extensive roof terrace. The horseshoe arches provide an appropriate neo-Moorish note to this pleasant establishment. Breakfast 25dh. If full, they'll send you on to the nearby *Hotel Essaouira*, much simpler but same management.

C Hotel Sherazade, 3 Derb Djama (3rd narrow street on your left as you head south down Riad Zitoun el Kedim from Jemaâ el Fna, big awning over door), **T** 044-429305, sherazade@iam.net.ma. *(29) Map 3, E7, p253* Germano-Moroccan management, English spoken. Spotlessly clean. Varied accommodation around large, pleasantly decorated courtyards. Rooftop terraces where breakfast is served. Can organize excursions and car hire. A popular address – reservations essential. Much more than a cheap hotel, but not exclusive and pricey like a riad. Avoid top floor rooms in summer.

Guéliz

A Hotel Le Méridien N'fis, intersection Av de France and Av de la Menara, **T** 044-339400, www.lemeridien.com. *(30) Map 4, L5, p255* The former Hotel N'fis (named for an Atlas river), beautifully revamped by the Méridien group. Pool, sauna, hammam, earth tennis courts, restaurants. Easily accessible, comfortable, highly recommended if you want a standard, no surprises, upscale hotel.

A Hotel Sheraton, intersection Av de France and Av de la Menara, **T** 044-448998. *(31) Map 4, L5, p255* Well-established tour- group hotel with all usual facilites, including a heated pool and piano bar. Has a loyal clientèle. Like the Méridien, a short taxi-ride from the médina.

A Villa Hélène, 89 Blvd Moulay Rachid, **T** 044-431681, also via Paris 0033-143204181, www.villahelene.com. *(32) Map 4, D4, p254* A large 1930s villa in a garden, a survival of the days when Guéliz was a cité-jardin. Nice pool. French-managed. Small apartment of 80 sq m available. Whole house can be rented in summer, sleeps up to 10. Excellent Moroccan meals to order.

B Hotel El Andalous, Av du Président-Kennedy, **T** 044-448228, resandalous@wanadoo.net.ma. *(33) Map 4, J5, p255* Nice, slightly worn hotel in a quiet corner of the Hivernage. Restaurants (including tapas bar *La Casa Latina*), pool. Popular with tour-groups as well as individual regulars.

C Hotel Ibis-Moussafir, Av Hassan II, Place de la Gare, **T** 044-435929. *(34) Map 4, F1, p254* Doubles at 500dh. Well-managed Ibis hotel with bar, restaurant and small pool, right next to the main train station. Go for a room overlooking the garden, as far as possible from the lifts. Sound-proofing problems were supposed to have been fixed during the last refit.

C-E **Résidence Gomassine**, 71 Blvd Mohammed Zerktouni, **T** 044-438454. *(35) Map 4, B3, p254* Well-located block of self-catering flats in the heart of Guéliz. Smallest double clocks in at 200dh. People opting for a longer stay can get better rates. Some flats have a balcony, air conditioning, all have satellite TV. (The Hotel Boustan over the street is best avoided.)

C/D **Hotel du Pacha**, 33 Rue de la Liberté, **T** 044-431327. *(36) Map 4, B4, p254* Hotel with restaurant not far from the Marché de Guéliz. Some rooms with air conditioning. A little rundown but a handy fall-back address. For quiet, specify a room *'côté cour'*.

C/D **Hotel Tafoukt**, Place du Petit Marché, Route de Targa (off plan), **T** 044-435510, h.tafoukt.rak@wanadoo.net.ma. *(37) Map 1, A1, p248* Small, gay-friendly hotel on the Targa road, fine if you have a car. Spacious rooms, including triple and quadruple suites. Satellite TV, air conditioning and refrigerator in rooms.

C/D **Hotel Jnene el Harti**, 30 Rue Qadi Ayyad, near main Guéliz post office, **T** 044-448000. *(38) Map 4, E3, p254* Modern building, rooms with air conditioning and TV. Best rooms on each side are 'the sevens' (107 etc). Popular with less well-off young Moroccans in Marrakech for the weekend. Maintenance not what it should be.

D **Hotel Oudaya**, 147 Rue Mohammed El Beqqal, **T** 044-448512. *(39) Map 4, B1, p254* As you face the Cinéma Colisée, go left and take first right. City hotel, typical of those built in the 1990s. Used by *Panorama* and other tour operators. 15 suites, 77 rooms, small unheated pool, restaurant and bar. Very clean. Pool-side rooms quietest. Fine for a couple of nights.

C/D Hotel Tachfine, corner of Blvd Zerktouni, almost next to Cinéma Colisée, entrance on side street, **T** 044-447188, tachfine@iam.net.ma. *(40) Map 4, B2, p254* Standard city hotel of no particular charm, handy when all other options fail. Restaurant on ground floor and snack restaurant across street from entrance. Location convenient for all services in Guéliz.

D Résidence El Hamra, 26 Av Mohammed V, **T** 044-448423, 044-448423. *Apartment block at the top end of Av Mohammed V, just opposite the Shell station.* *(41) Map 4, A1, p254* (**NB** Unwilling to take phone reservations!) Slightly run-down accommodation in the form of small one-bedroom flats with one bed in living area. Good size bathrooms, kitchen with fridge, gas ring but little else. Small pool at the back. Go for a quiet room *côte cour* (overlooking the back). Some rooms have been redone with pastel stucco-work – it's rather like sleeping inside a Turkish delight. Old fashioned air conditioning in some bedrooms. A vaguely gay address which is also popular with Moroccan families back from Europe in summer.

D/E Hotel Toulousain, 44 Rue Tarak Ibnou Ziad, **T** 044-430033. *(42) Map 4, C4, p254* Essential to reserve in advance. Popular hotel around two large patios. (Good breakfast served in patio with big palm tree). Has 32 rooms in all, many on the dark side, including around half with en suite shower. Car and bike parking which closes at 2300. Top floor rooms hot in summer.

F Hotel Farouk, 66 Av Hassan II, near the main post office, **T** 044-431989. *(43) Map 4, E3, p254* A long-established Marrakech address, same management as *Hotel Ali*. Acceptable at a pinch.

F Hotel Franco-Belge, 62 Blvd Mohammed Zerktouni, **T** 044-448472. *(44) Map 4, B2, p254* A bit rundown but practical. Go for rooms at the back opening onto the courtyard planted with orange trees. Seven rooms have en suite showers and loos. An establishment surviving from the days when Guéliz was something of a backwater. How long till it gets swallowed up by some promoter?

G YHA/Auberge de Jeunesse, Rue el Jehid, **T** 044-447713. *(45) Map 4, H1, p255* Handy for the station and amiably managed. (They'll even advise on setting up trips to Rissani and the Southeast). Boys on ground floor, girls first floor. Rooms sleep 4, 5 or 6 people.Try to reserve as capacity is limited in the smaller rooms. One YHA membership card essential. Hot showers extra. Buses for Guéliz and the médina and share taxis from outside the railway station. If time is limited, prefer a cheap hotel near Rue Bab Agnaou.

The Palmeraie

AL Amanjena Resort, Route de Ouazazate km 12, **T** 044-403353. Upscale complex centring on a large reflecting pool (*bassin*). Four types of accommodation, all luxuriously appointed with TV/DVD and CD players and big beds. Prices per night for 2 persons: pavilion, 6,950dh; pavilion with view of bassin, 8,000dh; maison with private pool, 15,000dh; maison jardin, also with private pool, 18,000dh. (The master bedrooms in the maison category are upstairs.) This is the first *Aman Resort* in Africa. Amanjena (says the blurb) comes from the Sanskrit *aman*, meaning peace, and the Arabic *jena*, meaning paradise. For the moment, it's all a bit new. The grounds – few mature trees – are disappointing. If you can afford these prices you'd be better off staying in a riad (or having your own). Popular with Saudis entertaining starlets and others in need of a certain discreetness (ie well out of town). 2 restaurants with stratospheric prices. On top of the prices there's a 10% service charge and 10% government tax.

AL Dar Sedra, Douar Abiad, near Les Deux Tours, reservations **T** 0033-146570087, www.dar-sedra.com. Simple villa, cream-yellow washed arcades next to pool, lawns and shade trees. Full house for rent at an extortionate €2,300 a night (5 rooms). Whole property sleeps up to 14. Not the top address, and for this kind of money it ought to be, but if you're having trouble finding somewhere and have a hole burning in your wallet it's worth bearing in mind.

AL Dar Tamsna, and the new **Jnane Tamsna**, reservations **T** 044-329423, 329884, **T** 06-1242717, www.tamsna.com. Same management as the beautiful *Riad Tamsna* eatery boutique in the médina. Well away from the bustle of downtown Marrakech, the twin villas (10 suites) of Dar Temsna make an ideal base if you have the funds. Close to the Palmeraie golf course. Highly personalized service, preferable to the industrial scale Amanjena. Available are organic food, tennis courts, pools and massages – you are definitely 'at home in the oasis'. Can set up tailor-made excursions with an ecological focus up into the mountains. One of the best addresses in Marrakech, much heralded by the likes of Condé-Nast Traveller.

A Dar Faracha, **T** 044-313901, www.atlas-sahara-trek.com. A very pleasant low villa with arcaded veranda, in a remote corner of the Palmeraie, with a pool and garden. Sleeps 6 to 8, rental 6,500dh/night. Calm and elegant (no haute decor here) without being minimalist. The owner, a native of Casablanca, knows the High Atlas and the southeastern deserts extremely well. Highly recommended – a good alternative to Dar Tamsna.

A Kasbah des Roses, km 9 route de Ouazarzate, **T** 044-329305, kasbahdesroses@iam.net.ma. 1 room and 3 suites in private pink concrete farmhouse on a 35-ha flower farm east of the city. Small pool. Owners will tell you all about growing roses. A little expensive for what's on offer.

A Les Deux Tours, out at Douar Abiad in the Palmeraie, about 1 km from the *Hotel Issil Club*, **T** 044-329525, www.deux-tours.com.

Double room starts at about 1,750dh a night, breakfast extra. Pick-up at Marrakech airport. Taxis will have difficulty finding this place, off a piste leading off the Palmeraie Circuit. Out in the palm groves, this small development was originally designed by local architect Charles Boccara as weekend retreats for Casablancans tired of the big smoke. The small houses, built in the vernacular tradition, are surrounded by palms, and each has its own plunge pool. There's also a good private hammam and swimming pool – it's all very fashion-shoot...except for the dodgy plumbing and the flies in summer (don't forget, you are in the middle of a working oasis). Meals available to order.

A **Palais Rhoul**, Dar Tounsi, Route de Fès, km 6, **T** 044-329494, www.palaisrhoul.com. Along with the Amanjena, this is the Hollywood end of Marrakech accommodation. Las Vegas meets Louis-Farouk decor and it's therefore not for the faint hearted. Suites open directly onto a colonnade surrounding a pool and there's a hammam. Whole palace can be rented, sleeping 20-plus people.

A **Palmeraie Golf Palace**, Les Jardins de la Palmeraie, 15 km from airport and 10 km from train station, **T** 044-301010. A 77-ha site, 314 rooms. Accommodation includes 6 senior suites, 2 royal suites and 24 suites with sitting room. All rooms have balcony, air conditioning, telephone, satellite TV, and 24-hr room service. Also on offer are restaurants, bars, baby sitter, crèche, travel agency, bank, hairdresser, laundry/dry cleaning, car rental, tennis, golf course, bowling, squash, horse riding, gym, hammam, 5 pools (2 heated – daily fee 200dh), conference centre and shopping arcade. It's all a bit overblown. If you're paying this sort of money, why not go for an upmarket riad and make sure they can lay on transport to the golf courses?

B/C **Tikida Garden**, Circuit de la Palmeraie, **T** 044-329595. Listed here in case you can't get into a riad or *Les Deux Tours*. Good pool, generally heated in winter.

Up the Amizmiz road

A Tigmi in Douar Tagadert, at 24 km turn-off on the Amizmiz road, near Kasbah Oumnast, **T** 06-1124422, www.tigmi.com. Remote, phoneless Tigmi hides smooth simplicity behind thick adobe walls in a poverty-stricken village. Inside: 8 suites, pool, food and wine, relaxation and views over the drought-stricken rolling landscape. A suite here will knock you back 3,000dh. Hire car necessary to nip into Marrakech or up to the mountains. For honeymooners or those rebuilding a relationship?

B/C Boughdira, located down a piste, 4 km after the Mobil station near the intersection of the Taroudant and Amizimiz routes, **T** 06-1173623. Traditional, and not in a chic way, simple guest house set in a big olive grove, with a pool and a warm welcome from owners Michèle and Youssef.

C Ferme d'accueil, off the Amizmiz road near Tamesloht; as you approach Tamesloht, look out for yellow signs, **T** 06-1342837. The smallholding is run on a sustainable basis by Myriem and Mustapha Nassef. They have 2 small guest chalets and will be operating their venture as an educational farm.

C/D Relais du Lac, on the shores of the Lalla Takerkoust dam, signposted a few kilometres before Amizmiz, **T** 044-484924. Accommodation for up to 20 people in small, country-style bungalows (370dh per person B&B, 500dh full board). Ideal for kids – lawns where they can run around on next to the lake – combined with 3 nights in a riad in Marrakech. In the neighbouring restaurant area, the Relais also has 185 places in traditional tents and caters for weddings and incentive business groups. Mountain biking, trekking and canoeing can be set up. The lake has shrunk a bit due to drought in recent years.

Up the Taroudant road

A Val de la Roseraie, Ouirgane, BP 769, **T** 044-439128. A peaceful resort (23 air-conditioned rooms) in extensive gardens, with 2 restaurants, bar, hammam, hydrotherapy centre, tennis, horse riding, outdoor pool and small indoor pool. Well-established clientèle. It's a little on the expensive side for the level of services on offer and the food is variable but it's still best upmarket option in the mountains.

B/C Auberge Au Sanglier Qui Fume, Ouirgane, CP 42150, **T** 044-485707/08. Small inn run by a French couple, the Poucets, the daughter and son-in-law of the people who founded the auberge back in 1945. Has 22 individually decorated chalet-style rooms, a restaurant serving excellent French country food, a bar, tennis and a pool in the summer. Would make a nice stop-off for a family. Mountain bikes available for rent, and the management will put you in touch with guides to take you hill-walking. Horse riding by arrangement with the neighbouring *Roseraie*.

C/D La Bergerie, about 2 km before Ouirgane village as you come from Marrakech, turn off right for Marigha, signposted, French management, **T** 044-485716, www.passionmaroc.com. Postal address BP 64 Marrakech. Gîte with 8 rooms in a farm-type atmosphere and set in 5 ha of grounds in a valley away from the village. Around 800dh/2 persons with breakfast, meal without wine at 150dh. Highly recommended. Better value than the Roseraie.

D Auberge Le Mouflon, Ouirgane, **T** 044-485722, 06-8944724. Options for sleeping are a single bungalow room or sleeping bags under a traditional tent. Pleasant setting, a good cheap option.

D Chez Momo, Ouirgane, **T** 044-485704, 06-1582295. (**NB** reservations unreliable). Simple country accommodation (2 small rooms, 2 2-room suites and 2 small suites). Mountain views. Fine for the price. Owner sometimes difficult to reach, even on his mobile. Good catering. Will be moving to a new setting in the area as a dam lake is set to modify the landscape somewhat.

Imlil and Toubkal

B/D La Kasbah de Toubkal, Imlil, **T** 044-485611, www.kasbahdu toubkal.com, (UK office: *Discover Ltd*, Timbers, Godstone RH9 8AD, **T** 0044-1883744392). The kasbah, which played the role of a Tibetan fortress in the recent film *Kundun*, has dormitory-type accommodation much-used by student groups, and a couple of very nice rooms on the terrace. The building, one-time HQ of the local caïd, has been well restored and for a 20dh contribution to the local development fund, you can have mint-tea and walnuts on the roof terrace. Food, too, but no alcohol.

D/E Atlas Gîte, Imlil, **T** 044-485609, manager Jean-Pierre Fouilloux. A good choice with 2 mini-apartments, 3 double rooms and 2 larger rooms. Home cooking and advice on setting up treks. 2 persons/300dh. Also does dormitory accommdation, 65dh/head.

E Hotel-Café El Aïne, as you arrive in Imlil from Asni on your right. Has 10 rudimentary rooms, the best ones upstairs. Meals to order.

G Refuge du Club Alpin Français, dormitory space for 30 people, at US$5 per night. Often crowded. On the plus side, the warden sells bottled water, soft drinks, and can do food for small groups. Campers using the level site below the hut can also use the facilities here.

Ourika Valley and Oukaïmeden

B-C La Ferme Berbere, along the Ourika road, 9 km from Marrakech, **T** 044-335685, 07-02726410, www.laferme-berbere.com. Country accommodation run by Jean-Louis and

Patricia. Its simple but very pleasant. They have 5 rooms, all with a fireplace. Outside, you can sleep under a nomad tent which has modern wash and loo facilities housed in sort of igloos made from adobe (the traditional country people's hammam). There's a small pool and good food. It's also a nice place for kids: there's a TV room with play station and lots of books and games. A whole week costs 3,500-5,500dh per room.

C Le Maquis, just before the roadside settlement of Oulmès, **T** 044-484531. With Franco-Moroccan management, *Le Maquis* has both proper guest rooms (1 person 260dh with breakfast) and 6-sleeper bunk rooms. Accommodation here is bright and cheerful, the restaurant slightly less so (basic menus 55-120dh).

D Hotel de l'Angour (aka *Auberge Chez Juju*), Oukaïmeden, **T** 044-319005, reservations via Marrakech **T** 044-448378. Open all year (except Ramadan). Hotel with 8 rooms, a fair restaurant with basic European cooking, a bar with cold beer, half-pension required (250dh). Fair prices for clean sheets and hot showers.

E Auberge Ramuntcho, **T** 044-444521, 06-1165182, at km 50 from Marrakech. 14 nice-sized rooms, 2 persons 300dh, 1 person 250dh, breakfast 40dh. Set up by a Basque – hence the name, Ramuntcho being 'king of the mountains' in a Pierre Loti novel. The large (too large?) restaurant (pleasant outside terrace) hosts a lot of lunchtime tour groups. Bar and small pool.

E Dar Piano, Oulmès, **T** 044-484842, 06-1342884, darpiano@ wanadoo.net.ma. Closed Jun-Aug. Four chintzy, cosy rooms at 200dh per person or 250dh for 2. Breakfast 40dh. Also a small flat sleeping 4 for 400dh. The restaurant has a good menu at 150dh. (**NB** This Oulmès not to be confused with Oulmès-les-Thermes, between Meknès and Rabat, where the fizzy water comes from.)

G Hotel Billa, Setti Fatma, right at the top end of the village, on the right, after the crossing to the cascades. Probably the best of numerous cheap hotels here. 20 rooms, 60dh/1 person, breakfast 20dh, hot shower 10dh. Large *salon marocain* with river view.

Camping Amassine, after the pottery on the road from Dar Caïd Ourika to Setti Fatma; there is a sign. A woody (peach trees) and apparently secure site with room for camping cars. Charges, 9dh tent, 8dh person, 8dh hot shower.

Tizi-n-Tichka road (with Telouet)

C Maison d'hôte l'Roccha, 25 km after Igherm, on the south-facing side of the Atlas, between Telouet and Aït Ben Haddou turn-offs. A fine traditional mountain house, about 1 km down a piste from the road. Clean, slightly stylish rooms opening off courtyard, all with hot water. Mediterranean and local food. A good address on this road.

D Maison d'hôte Afoulki, Telouet, not far from the central market place, **T** 044-890714, jkevork@yahoo.fr. Small traditional house, French-owned, with 4 rooms and 2 bathrooms. Basic meals possible (tajines and the like), around 70dh a head. Probably best to soldier on to Ouarzazate, unless you're counting on doing some tramping hereabouts.

D/E Auberge de Telouet, drive through Telouet village, as if heading for the Glaoui kasbah, **T** 044-890717, 06-2134455. Six rooms, also option of kipping out on terrace in a sleeping bag.

Essaouira

Essaouira now has good number of restored properties operated as guest houses. The typical old house rises up two storeys round a courtyard with rooms opening onto balconies round all four sides. If the courtyard is small, the result is often a bit gloomy to modern western taste (although high ceilings and decoration schemes compensate for this). **NB** It is important to reserve accommodation during the annual Gnaoua Festival.

A Baoussala, 8 km south of Essaouira at El Ghazoua, heading south from Essaouira on Agadir road, at Km 8 look out for marker on your right, you reach Baoussala after 3km of track, (10 km to surf-spot), **T** 044-474345, 06-6308746, www.baoussala.com. Purpose-built guesthouse in peaceful, extensive grounds with tall eucalyptus trees. Has 4 en suite rooms built around a circular open living space. Managed by owners Dominique and Bruno Maté. Prices 650dh per head, whole house can be rented. Meals to order, half-board for stays over 5 days.

B Dar Loulema, 2 Rue Souss, **T** 044-475346, 06-1247661, www.darloulema.com. *(1) Map 5, C2, p256* Centrally situated next to the the Café Taros. 6 rooms with air conditioning, 1 with bath. Roof terraces overlook the big square, the port and the old town. Each room is named for a Moroccan city and decorated accordingly. Meals to order. The French owners have spent years in the country.

B Sofitel Essaouira, Av Mohammed V, **T** 044-479000. A comfortable Accor hotel, opposite the beach, just what the town needed. Pleasant enough bar (which could be anywhere, however) and a good restaurant. Also has a thalassotherapy centre.

B/C Hotel Palazzo Desdemona, Av Okba ibn Nafi, **T** 044-472227. *(2) Map 5, D5, p256* Prices run from 500dh for simplest room on terrace to 950dh for a suite. Fireplaces in some rooms, plenty of hot water, but has had poor reviews regarding its service. No food available apart from breakfast. Same management as the much- photographed *Auberge Tangaro*, see below.

B/C Hotel Villa Maroc, 10 Rue Abdallah ben Yassin, **T** 044-476147, villamaroc@casanet.net.ma. *(3) Map 5, D2, p256* Major credit cards accepted. Converted merchant's house with 17 rooms focusing on a central court festooned with plants and greenery, roof terrace with superb views, apartment sleeping 4 available for 1,200dh, restaurant for guests only, dinner 150dh, breakfast included in room price, public parking nearby on Place Orson Welles. A personable establishment but a victim of its own success. Hot water for showers can be a problem if several people are showering at the same time.

C Auberge Tangaro, Diabat, **T** 044-784784. Same management as *Hotel Palazzo Desdemona* in town. Has 13 rooms and 5 suites, half-board (2 people 800dh) compulsory. A pleasant farm-type place. No electricity, good food, hot water a bit dodgy sometimes. Evening meals by candlelight. Reception not what it could be. Suite 6 has good ocean view. Camping sometimes possible.

C Casa del Mar, 35 Rue d'Oujda, **T** 044-475091, 06-8943839, www.lacasa-delmar.com. *(4) Map 5, B4, p256* Attractive, simple house with a crisp, Hispanic feel (the owners are from Mallorca). Has 4 rooms with shower on 2 levels around a narrow patio. Fine ocean views from roof terrace. Meals to order. Highly recommended.

C Hotel Jasira, 18 Rue Moulay Ali Cherif, Quartier des Dunes, **T** 044-784403, aljasira@iam.net.ma. 30 rooms and 4 small suites, pool, restaurant, but no booze. Prices in the 400-500dh bracket.

C Hotel Tafoukt, 98 Av Mohammed V, BP 38, **T** 044-784504/05. A reasonable hotel with 40 rooms (make sure you ask for one with a sea view), just across the road from the beach but an appreciable walk (about 1 km) from the centre of town. Tea room, bar and restaurant.

C Riad Gyvo, 3 Rue Mohammed ben Messaoud, **T** 044-475102, 06-1686156, www.riadgyvo.com. *(5) Map 5, D3, p256* Three studios (ground floor ones on dark side), 2 small flats with cooking facilities, roof terrace. Wonderful views from the *garçonnière* up on the roof. Planted patio flanked with stone columns. Impeccably kept. Mini-weights room, if you really must whilst you're on holiday.

C The Tea House, 74 Derb Laâlouj, La Skala, reservations on **T** 044-783543, www.aescalon.demon.co.uk/teahouse. Despite its English name, this small guesthouse is very much 'traditional Essaouira'. Two self-catering 5-room flats are available for rent, beautifully decorated, each accommodating 4 people. Each flat has kitchen, large bathroom, living/dining room with open fire (a definite draw) and 2 bedrooms. Breakfast included, along with firewood. Recommended.

C Villa Argana , about 11 km from Essaouira at Ghazoua on the Sidi Kaouki road, look out for a turn left, **T** 044-474365, 06-1618532. Around 600dh for two. Three eccentrically pleasing rooms with a cave-like feel. On the expensive side. No electricity as yet. English-owned.

C/D Hotel Villa Soleil, Plage de Sidi Kaouki, 15 km from Essaouira, **T** 044-474763, 07-0233097, www.hotelvillasoleil.com. Nine simple rooms and 1 suite, 300dh single, 800dh suite for 4 people. A good basic address that feels like a sort of whitewashed village. Possibly better in off-season. Meals from 100dh. A mini-suite on the roof has ocean view.

D/E Auberge de la Plage, Sidi Kaouki, **T** 044-476600. Italo-German management, 11 rooms, 250dh-350dh double. Shared showers and loos. No electricity (yet). More importantly, they do horse riding and camel excursions.

D/E Hotel el Andalous, as you leave bus station, cross over main road towards the pharmacy, hotel is on the avenue on right, **T** 044-472951. Preferable to *Palais d'Essaouira* if you need quiet and there's a café on ground floor. 1 person 150dh, 2 people 250dh, 3 people 300dh.

E Hotel Palais d'Essaouira, 5 Av du 2 Mars, right opposite the bus station, **T** 044-472887. Hotel with much Moroccan decoration and 29 rooms, some triples, opening onto central, covered courtyard. Very clean but noisy at night if the TV's on in central area. Restaurant on the ground floor.

F Chez Brahim, 41 Rue el Mourabitine, near Bab Marrakech, **T** 044-472599. *(6) Map 5, C6, p256* A very good budget option. Prices tend to be negotiable, around 80dh for a single, breakfast 15dh. Clean establishment, rooms around a courtyard, pleasant terrace for breakfast. One of Brahim's scouts meets likely guests at the Supratours bus stop or the bus station. Room for surfboards on ground floor. No sign, you get the house keys to let yourself in.

Self-catering accommodation   Jack's Kiosk, at 1 Place Prince Moulay El Hassan, **T** 044-475538. **Essaouira Médina**, **T** 044-472396, www.essaouiramedina.com. More upmarket and they also have a good name if you are interested in buying property.

Safi

D Hotel Atlantide, Rue Chaouki, **T** 044-462160/1. No credit cards. Quiet position overlooking the centre of Safi new town, close to the *Hotel Safir* (to which it is to be entirely preferred). Has 47 rooms, a pleasant restaurant with terrace and a nice pool. An Agatha Christie sort of place with an air of faded elegance not entirely wrecked by recent renovation work. Opened in 1920 by the Compagnie Paquet de Navigation as the *Hotel Marhaba*, the

Atlantide now belongs to the Office Chérifien des Phosphates, and is mostly used by company personnel (lots of seminars). Rooms plain but comfortable, some have panoramic views. Next door is the *Cinema Atlantide* offering one daily afternoon film performance for hotel guests, parking in quiet street.

E Hotel Assif, Av de la Liberté, **T** 044-622940. 60 rooms, clean and comfortable (250dh per 2 persons with shower), family rooms available, breakfast 20dh, restaurant, street parking in front of hotel, lift, TV and telephone.

G Hotel Majestic, Place de l'Indépendence (corner of Av Moulay Youssef), clearly visible from main square next to the médina, **T** 044-464011. Has 20 rooms, triple 110dh, shared showers 5dh, TV room. Basic but quite friendly and clean. No breakfast. Public parking 20 m.

G Hotel/Café de l'Avenir, **T** 044-462657. Round the corner and up a side street from the Majestic, a gloomy but useful address, tiny restaurant at back, hot shower shared, 5dh, cold showers in rooms with WC.

G Hotel de Paris, **T** 044-462149. Further up the street from the Majestic, on the right. Clean, big, airy rooms (1 person 30dh, 2 people 60dh), in an old house built round a courtyard. More Spartan than this would be difficult to find.

Oualidia

B/C Hotel Hippocampe, **T** 023-366108. Small, very relaxed hotel with 20 rooms. Popular restaurant, bar, tennis and immaculate pool, beautiful setting above lagoon. Check is half-board is compulsory.

E Motel-Restaurant à l'Araigneé Gourmande, **T** 023-366447 (important to reserve). Hotel with 15 rooms, all with balconies, 6 with ocean view (2 people 290dh half board), good restaurant particularly for fish, street parking, welcoming staff, slight damp smell, dining room a bit gloomy but terrace views of the lagoon, royal villa, recommended. Cheap menu 70dh, 200dh menu with lobster. Half-board compulsory.

E Hotel Restaurant l'Initiale T 023-366246, opened late 2000. Six spacious rooms (2 persons 200dh) near ocean, 1 with ocean view in a very clean and charming hotel. Good Italian menu at 90dh, other menu at 180dh.

Eating and drinking

Moroccans proudly assert that their cooks produce one of the four great cuisines of the world (the others being Chinese, French and Indian). An extreme claim, perhaps, but Marrakech is winning culinary credentials, and there is interesting food for all budgets. Everywhere you'll find the Moroccan national standards, couscous and *tagjine* (meat and seasonal vegetables slow cooked on a brazier), plus other more subtle dishes. *Tanjia* (lamb slow-baked in a clay pot) is the local speciality (see p134).

In old Marrakech, options range from street-side barbecues to diet-destroying gourmet banquets in a palatial setting. A new breed of boutique restaurants serves a makeover version of Moroccan food: all the staples with Levantine, Italian and Gallic grace-notes. Service will be kindly and attentive and the freshness of the ingredients makes for fine-flavoured food.

In Essaouira, the choice of eateries is similar to Marrakech but with an emphasis of fish. In the mountains, expect to eat a lot of *tajine*. However, beware of salads and fresh fruit in the cheaper restaurants. Hygiene is not always what it should be.

₸₸₸	More exclusive places, often with a French touch, also Marrakech 'palace' restaurants serving 5- or 6-course banquets. 200dh and over.
₸₸	A 'proper' restaurant with most of the trappings. A main dish and drink for starting at 50dh, a full feed for anything between 70dh and 200dh.
₸	Light meals and snacks, a good feed for under 50dh.

You may want to try the blow-out Marrakchi dining experience in all its six course splendour. After *harira* soup or a selection of salads, you'll be served a 'yellow' dish, possibly chicken *m'qalli*, couscous, *bastilla* (filo-pastry pie with pigeon, egg and almonds) and possibly steamed lamb. Afters may include *jaouhara* (fried filo pastry with a cream), *kab ghzal*, 'gazelle horns' or a palate-cleaning orange and cinnamon salad.

The traditional banquet generally includes some sort of 'entertainment', ranging from the discrete tinkling of a lutist to the plaintive cries and thrumming of gnaoua musicians. A *danseuse orientale* often makes her entrance just in time for dessert, and it is traditional for the most ungainly Caucasian male to be dragged from his seat to perform. If the full banquet experience doesn't appeal (cost generally between 550dh and 800dh, with wine), then there are plenty of restaurants which have à la carte menus.

NB When dining out in a 'palace' restaurant, make the reservations yourself, if possible. Travel agencies and other intermediaries make large commissions, often as much as 30% of the price of a meal. If the restaurant seems to be in the depths of the médina, ask where you'll be met or what you need to tell the taxi driver.

Interesting salads excepted, **vegetarians** get a raw deal. Practically all main dishes are cooked with meat, an ingredient so central to the culture that for most Moroccans being vegetarian is hardly conceivable. (The main religious holiday, Aïd el Kebir, centres on the ritual sacrifice of a sheep or goat.) In your average restaurant, serving a vegetarian couscous means taking the meat off the top. Be prepared to eat lots of omelettes and processed cheese but enjoy such delights as *aubergine zaâlouk*, grilled pepper and tomato salad and *bissara* (bean soup).

Jemaâ el Fna and around

Restaurants

♦♦♦ **Les Jardins de la Koutoubia**, 26 Rue de la Koutoubia, **T** 044-388800. *1230-1600, 1930-1030. Credit cards accepted. Map 3, D5, p252* Although the building is a brand new concrete riad, the pool-side restaurant terrace is good for lunch – and a welcome relief from the traffic outside. Salads and pasta with alcohol, handy if you're hungry after snapping away on 'la Place'.

♦♦ **Les Terrasses de l'Alhambra**, sort of opposite the Hotel de France at the Derb Debbachi side of the square (about as far as you can get from the Koutoubia). *0800 till late. Map 3, C7, p253* A new outfit run by a team from Toulouse. Café and ices downstairs, salads, pizza and pasta upstairs. Makes a good change from tajine and won't break the bank. Air-conditioned interior.

♦♦ **Restaurant de l'Hotel de France**, Jemaâ el Fna. *1200-2200. Map 3, D7, p253* Something of an institution, was here long, long before many of the trendy places. The street-level terrace enables you to keep a close eye on the flow of people between 'La Place' and Derb Debbachi, the roof terraces have super views. On the menu? Simple basics.

▶ Berber whisky

Chance is that after a successful round of negotiations for a carpet, the bazariste will clap his hands and bellow "*ETTEY*". 'Ah, le whisky berbère', grins your friendly carpet merchant, supping at this nectar from China. In fact, any occasion is good for tea – *ettey* is so central to Moroccan life that it comes as a shock to realize that it has only been commonly available since the 19th century.

Moroccan tea is of the green gunpowder variety and is generally served in a glass stuffed with mint leaves (*enaânaâ*). Never too strong, the basic version of the drink is like liquid polo mint. Theatrically, the pourer raises and lowers the *berrad* (tea pot) to generate foam on the surface of the tea.

Ettey is varied according to the season with fragrant herbs. For each time of year, there is a flavour. *Fleyou*, peppermint, warms the body while dried *louiza* or verbena is more medicinal. Sage, marjoram and orange flowers are also used.

Every neighbourhood has its official *moul'ikama* or mint seller. Arriving early in the morning, he sets up shop in the shade of a wall. Bright green leafy bundles are laid elegantly on a piece of sacking. But while tea in the city often means artful herbal compositions, among nomads the drink is different altogether. Bedouin tea is dark and very sweet, slow boiled in a tiny pot in the embers of a brasero.

Old Moroccan families treasure tea implements handed down the generations. There will be a mallet used for breaking up the sugar loaves, now a thing of the past. The metal berrad will bear the mark of a factory in Manchester. In fact, tea came to Morocco via the English. With the Russian Empire off limits during the 1854 Crimean War, British merchants sought new markets in Morocco. The fashion for tea soon spread, perhaps building on an old tradition of herbal infusions. Tea joined milk and dates at the heart of Moroccan hospitality.

♔Y Restaurant de l'Hotel Ali, Rue Moulay Ismaïl. *Map 3, E6, p252* Part of the hotel of the same name. The food is unexceptional but we've listed it here as a place to meet up with trekkers and others who've been roughing it round Morocco.

♔Chegrouni, a no-name place, a few paces from the restaurant of *L'Hotel de France*, identifiable by its terrace gallery on which lunchers sit lined up looking onto the street. *Map 3, C8, p253* A good feed for 50dh. Gets crowded with visitors and locals. Arrive early, this place is almost too popular for its own good.

♔Grill-restaurants, Rue Bani Marine, the street beginning on Jemaâ el Fna with an arch between the post office and Bank al Maghrib, then a moped-park. *Map 3, E6, p252* The best is probably **El Bahja**, next to the *Hotel La Gazelle*. Avoid salads but the meat is usually fresh.

Cafés and salons de thé

♔Café Argana, on the north side of Jemaâ el Fna, look out for sign. *Map 3, D7, p252* Quite a rendez-vous point for trendy, courting couples and tourists. Excellent pâtisseries and good view from terraces but the staff are often overwhelmed.

♔Café de la CTM, over the Hotel CTM, Jemaâ el Fna. *Map 3, D7, p252* When the Argana is packed, you can usually find a place to sit here. The clientèle tends towards the backpacker and young local rather than the well-heeled fashionista. Drinks and service very basic. For exceedingly good cakes you're better off at the Argana.

♔Café 'Lipton' (and others on the Rue Bab Agnaou). *Map 3, D6, p252* The pedestrian street starting with the palm trees and leading up to the *Hotel Tazi* has several strategic cafés for people-watching.

Fresh from the country
Cooked garlic-free, even picky kids might chew on these snails.

♥ **Pâtisserie des Princes**, Rue Bab Agnaou. *Map 3, D6, p252*
Along with the *Pâtisserie Hilton* in Guéliz, a top pâtisserie address.
Discreet courting couples hide away in the tea-rooms upstairs,
locals come in to pick up their orders for parties and receptions. Fill
your face with *bastilla* here.

North of Jemaâ el Fna

Restaurants

♥♥♥♥ **Dar el Baroud**, Av Mohammed V, next to a chemist, on a side
street practically opposite the Koutoubia, **T** 044-426009. *1930-2230,
reservations. Map 3, D4, p252* Menu at 400dh or à la carte. All the
basics in pleasant neo-traditional surroundings. Not the top address.
Reliable but really for those without the time to seek out an eatery
deep in the médina.

▶ Tanjia Marrakchia

Ask Marrakchis what the city's most typical dish is and they'll tell you *tanjia*. Like tajine, the name comes from the container in which the food is cooked. A tanjia is a tall, glazed clay, amphora-like pot and all old Marrakchi families will have at least one. (Certain butchers will rent them or can have the dish cooked for you.)

Tanjia is really a male preserve. Prepared in the morning, the pot can be left to slow cook in the neighbourhood *koucha* (baker's oven), ready after a hard day's labour to eat with friends. Or it can be cooked in the heat of the hammam furnace ready for a football post-mortem. (These days, some people knock them up in a pressure cooker – although connoisseurs will tell you that it's not at all the same thing.) In its simplest version, the tanjia master will fill the pot with good-sized haunches of lamb (or camel), adding garlic and preserved lemon (an important ingredient in a number of

Moroccan stews), oil and water. Essential seasoning takes the form of ginger, saffron, cumin, black pepper and a touch of grated nutmeg – all apparently constituting something of an aphrodisiac brew.

The final touch to a tanjia is provided by a sprinkling of *ra's el hanout* (lit. 'the head of the shop'), your local grocer's favourite spice mixture. No Marrakchi kitchen would be complete without a bottle of this condiment, composed of at least seven heavily pounded ingredients, including cardamom, cinnamon, red pepper, saffron, and turmeric. Though traditionally-run Moroccan homes make their own spice mixtures, you can find ra's el hanout in any médina épicerie. A good tanjia will have just the right amount of water to ensure the meat doesn't burn. With too much water, you run the risk of producing deep boiled lamb rather than succulent meat, waiting to be pulled flaking off the bone.

¶¶¶ **Dar Fès**, 8 Rue Boussouni, Riad Laârous, **T** 044-382340, www.darfez.com. *Map 2, G5, p250* Run by one Chérif, a former chemist turned restaurateur. All the great Moroccan standards reliably produced here. Its big plus is greenery on a hot-house scale in the candle-lit patio. Large enough for small groups, Dar Fès has an intimate touch, too.

¶¶¶ **Le Fondouk**, 55 Rue souk Hal Fassi, Kaât Bennhadid, **T** 044-378190. *To get there, take a taxi to Moukef in the médina and get them to meet you. Around 200dh a head for a good feed. Map 3, A10, p253* The style-police approved this one, a former merchants' hostel (*fondouk*) converted into an upscale restaurant. Entrées: *bijou briouates* (little samosas). Pasta and fish brochettes for those tired of the inevitable *tajine*. Also serves good desserts. The roof terrace is open in summer and the designer loos are worth a trip.

¶¶¶ **Dar Marjana**, down an impasse just at the intersection of Rue Bab Doukkala and Rue Dar el Bacha, **T** 044-385110. *Evenings only, reservations essential. Map 2, H5, p250* 'The House of Coral' is one of the city's longest established 'traditional' restaurants. Tables outside in the garden patio or in one of the more intimate side rooms provide the setting for the full Moroccan dining experience. The owner, if too full of alcohol, can get more frisky than one would like with women diners. Gnaoua musicians and a gaudy belly dancer round off the desserts. Expect to pay about 650dh for the full whack, drinks included.

¶¶¶ **Dar Moha**, Rue Dar el Bacha, **T** 044-386400. *Lunchtimes and evenings, reservations preferable. Map 2, H5, p250* One of the first riads to 'go public', the former residence of Pierre Balmain now houses a médina palace restaurant frequented by well-heeled Marrakchis and expats. Lunchtime is very pleasant in the garden. It's an upscale eatery (despite the piped music) very worthy of attention. Try sword-fish *bastilla* or *tarte au zeste de mandarine*.

🍴🍴🍴 **Ksar Essaoussan**, Leksour neighbourhood, **T** 044-440632. *Closed Sun and Aug. Reservations essential.* Map 3, B5, p252 Along with Le Tobsil (see below), this place is rated as one of the Red City's top tables. The setting, a small 18th-century patrician home, contrasts with the Las Vegas dazzle of some of the médina places. The cooking is reliable, three menus (300-500dh) include a half-bottle of wine and mineral water. Possibly a little too intimate for some tastes. **NB** Photo opportunities from the terraces.

🍴🍴 **Le Pavillon**, 47 Derb Zaouia, Bab Doukkala, **T** 044-387040. *Evenings only, closed Tue and Aug.* Map 2, H3, p250 Around 450dh a head, à la carte, drinks included. Said to be the best French restaurant in Marrakech, the menu changing on a daily basis. The place for a little *terrine de sanglier*, or perhaps some *magret de canard au miel*. Dine inside or under the orange trees.

🍴🍴 **Le Tobsil**, Derb Abdallah ben Hussein, Leksour, **T** 044-444052, 044-441523. *Evenings only. Reservations essential.* Map 3, C5, p252 Moroccan standards cooked and served with more subtlety than is perhaps the norm. Sophisticated but can get a bit cramped (there are only a handful of tables). Hearing the next table's chat is fine in a Paris bistro, but perhaps not if you're being relieved of 600dh at the same time?

🍴🍴 **Yacout**, 79 Sidi Ahmed Soussi, **T** 044-382929. *Evenings only, closed Mon and Aug. Total 600dh, including apéritif, wines and digestif.* Map 2, F4, p250 A classic (although the cuisine is said to have declined in recent years following extension works), born of the fervid imagination of one Bill Willis, haut décorateur extraordinaire. Here are all the trappings of Marrakech style: tadelakt-slathered chunky walls, domes, candles and fireplaces, pierced metal lanterns and low cushioned banquettes. There's also a wonderful roof-terrace for drinks and al fresco dining next to a plunge pool. You may even be so blown away by the gorgeousness of it all that you won't notice the poverty in the alleys when you stumble out to find your waiting taxi.

Cafés

⛾ **Café du Musée de Marrakech**, Place Ben Youssef. *Map 3, A9, p253* Small café serving mint tea, soft drinks and a small selection of pastries. Perhaps its key advantages are its clean loos and the fact that you can allow kids to run around a bit without worrying about speeding mopeds. A useful halt between souks and the Medersa Ben Youssef and Dar Belarj. (You can visit the café without going into the museum.)

South of Jemaâ el Fna

Restaurants

⛾⛾⛾ **Riad Tamsna**, 23 Derb Zanka Daika, Riad Zitoun Jedid, **T** 044-385272, www.tamsna.com. *Open for lunch and till late, some credit cards accepted. Map 3, E8, p253* Certainly the most bijou address south of Jemaâ el Fna, the antithesis of the Berber-Baroque tourist-trap eateries. Light Lebano-Moroccan cuisine. Can't really be faulted. The place for drinks on the terrace with tapas at sundown.

⛾⛾⛾-⛾⛾ **Dar Mima**, Derb Zaouia el Kadriya, Riad Zitoun Kedim, not far from the Dar Si Said, **T** 044-385252. *Evenings only, closed Wed. Map 3, F9, p253* A la carte Moroccan eating for around 200dh. Popular with foreign residents. Portions said to be on the small side. Eat upstairs in one of the smaller *salons*.

⛾⛾ **Nid'Cigogne**, Place des Tombeaux-Saâdiens, **T** 044-443348. *Open daily for lunch. Map 1, H9, 249* The 'Stork's Nest' is a reliable little place for salads and *grillades* after soldiering round the museum neighbourhood. The big plus is the roof terrace with view of aforementioned *Cigogne's* domestic arrangements.

Guéliz

Restaurants

🍴🍴🍴 **Le Jacaranda**, 32 Blvd Mohammed Zerktouni (opposite *Café Les Négociants*), **T** 044-447215. *Closed Tue and Wed lunchtime. Map 4, B2, p254* Long-standing restaurant with good reputation. Elaborate French food, strong on fish and creamy sauces, bar. Eating à la carte, expect to pay 250dh. The menus are much cheaper. Terrace very noisy (and polluted, it's next to a busy traffic light), so sit upstairs inside for quiet. Occasional live music.

🍴🍴🍴 **La Trattoria**, 179 Rue Mohammed el Beqqal, **T** 044-432641, www.latrattoriamarrakech.com. To locate, find *La Taverne* (opposite Cinéma Le Colisée near rond-point Abd el Moumen), which is on corner of Blvd Zerktouni and Rue Mohammed el Beqqal. *La Trattoria* is 2 blocks down, near to *Café L'Amandine*. *Map 4, C2, p254* The soul of the original owner, the baroque Gian Carlo, hovers over this place and standards are maintained. Probably the city's best Italian restaurant with an excellent selection of wines and superb desserts.

🍴🍴 **Catanzaro**, Rue Tarak ibn Ziad, behind the market in Guéliz, next to the Hotel Toulousain, **T** 044-433731. *Reservation essential for the evening. Map 4, C4, p254* Excellent Italian food. Full meal for around 150dh, though you can spend far less. A very popular lunchtime address.

🍴🍴 **Chez Jack'line**, 63 Av Mohammed V, **T** 044-447547. *Map 4, B2, p254* Atmospheric, a 1950s bistro. Serves French and Italian cuisine which is ideal when you've just spent 2 weeks up in the mountains eating tagine. There is a resident parrot, too. The lion cub has long gone, sadly, as has the monkey. Jack'line soldiers on, a Marrakech original, in a Ronnie Corbet sort of way.

♕ La Conch, Rue Loubnène, not far from the Guéliz food market, **T** 044-436471. *Map 4, C4, p254* Basque specialities, tapas in a Basque-themed bar. All kind of exotic in a Marrakech setting.

♕ L'Entrecôte, 55 Blvd Zerktouni, **T** 044-449428, manager Abdel Ghani Khatir's mobile **T** 06-1245042. From the rond-point Abd el Moumen, facing *Les Négociants*, go left. *L'Entrecote* is on your right, about 20 m from the roundabout, in a courtyard building. *Map 4, B3, p254* Serves particularly good meat. Menu 120dh, lunchtime quick menu 70dh, 150dh for a good feed. Rather dark dining room best in evening but recommended nevertheless.

♕ Le Jardin des Arts, 6/7 Rue Sakia el Hamra, **T** 044-446634. Near the Hotel Amine and Café le Diamant Vert. In Semlalia rather than Guéliz (so you'll need to take a cab) but included here for convenience. A newish French restaurant that fills the gap in the Semlalia hotel zone. Said to be really quite good although some reports say it's overpriced.

♕ Odissea, 83 bis Blvd Mansour Eddahbi, **T** 044-431545. To get there, coming from the médina on Av Mohammed V, locate the main RAM agency and Wafa Bank. Go left, and left again. Odissea is a few metres down on your right. *Map 4, D2, p254* The decor of this Italian-run restaurant is *molto Versace*, with impeccable waistcoated waiters and giant paintings of leopards. Serves excellent pizzas. Pizza and wine for 2 will work out at about 200dh.

♕ Pizzeria Niagara, route de Targa (take a taxi), near the Petit Marché, **T** 044-449775. *Reservations essential. Map 1, B2, p248*

Good pizzas. Covered terrace. Gets crowded in the evenings with chic locals. Recommended.

⚭ **Rotisserie du Café de la Paix**, 68 Rue Yougoslavie, **T** 044-433118. *Map 4, D2, p254* Reasonable grilled food all the year round. And there's a garden in the summer.

⚭ **Restaurant Bagatelle**, 101 Rue Yougoslavie, just opposite the Rotisserie de la Paix, **T** 044-430274. *1200-1400 and 1900-2300. Closed on Wed. Map 4, D3, p254* Is to French food in Marrakech what *Catanzaro* is to Italian. Solid Gallic offerings served in the restaurant and vine-shaded courtyard. Decor 1940s kitsch with 1970s touches. Waiters like ageing bodyguards serve Inspecteur Maigret types coming in for a pleasant lunch (siesta required afterwards). Try the *salade fermier* or the *terrine de faisan au porc*. Recommended – good lunch for around 100dh, the full whack for 200dh.

⚭ **Tivoli**, Route de Casablanca, **T** 044-313528. *Out on the Casablanca road a short taxi hop from the new town – turn left just before you get to the Marjane Hypermarket if coming from Guéliz. Lunchtimes and evenings, closed Sun. Map 1, A2, p248* The decor is no great shakes, but local foreign residents rate the Italian cooking (anything for a change from tajine). Menu changes daily.

⚭ **Chez Bel Guéni**, and other no-name barbecue restaurants, go right at the top of Av Mohammed V, and heading along Av Khattabi, away from the Shell station, after the *Hotel Les Ambassadeurs*, you'll find a handful of lively *grillade* places. *Map 4, A1, p254* Worth discovering on a second trip to Marrakech.

⚭ **Café Agdal**, 86 Av Mohammed V, **T** 044-448707. *Map 4, B2, p254* Perfectly serviceable place with pavement terrace, close to Rond-Point Abd el Moumen, next to Hotel Moutamid. All basic meals, good breakfast (buy the papers at nearby news kiosk).

¶ **Tiffany**, under the arcade on Av Mohammed V, near the post office. *Map 4, D4, p254* Basic meals and breakfasts, good service, stays open during the day in Ramadan.

Cafés and salons de thé

¶ **Amandine**, 97 Rue Mohammed el Beqqal, **T** 044-449612. *0800-2030, closes in the afternoon, 1300-1600 during the week. Map 4, D2, p254* Clean, well-run salon de thé, a little more expensive than the run of the mill. For chocolate and pastries. Recommended.

¶ **Kenzemène**, Rue Mohammed el Beqqal, round corner from La Taverne. *Map 4, C2, p254* Very polite salon de thé where women can consume tea and pâtisseries unmolested. For refreshments during shopping therapy. Recommended.

¶ **Pâtisserie Belkabir**, Rue de la Liberté, on the corner with Rue Tarak Ibnou Ziad. *Map 4, B4, p254* A long-established traditional Moroccan cake-place. There is a similar establishment at the other end of Rue de la Liberté, near Côté Sud and other bijou boutiques.

¶ **Pâtisserie Hilton**, just off Rond-Point Abd el Moumen, on the pedestrian street. *Map 4, B2, p254* A top address for Moroccan petits-fours and the like. Get yourself a mini-pastilla for lunch (or afternoon snack). Gift-wrapped *pâtisseries* to take home. Definitely worth a look.

Up the Taroudant road

All the smaller settlements frequented by hikers – Imlil, Oukaïmeden, Setti Fatma – have plenty of cheap 'no-name' eateries serving tajine and *mechoui* (brochettes). Vegetarians may be lucky and get an omelette – or have to make do with bread, processed cheese and yoghurt. Hygiene standards are variable.

Those with weak stomachs should buy and wash their own fruit and vegetables and have a picnic.

Restaurants

🍴 Le Val de la Roseraie, Ouirgane BP 769, Marrakech 40000, **T** 044-439128. The Roseraie (see also p117) makes a welcome up-market lunch stop on the road up to Tin Mal. The food is variable but along with the nearby *Sanglier qui fume*, it's the last really comfy eatery before you get to Taroudant over the mountains.

🍴 Auberge Au Sanglier Qui Fume, Ouirgane, CP 42150, **T** 044-485707/08. 'The smoking wild boar', even figures (occasionally) on the menu. French country food and a bar. A reliable address, typical of a fast-disappearing sort of restaurant. Once upon a time, there were licensed auberge-ish type places like this across Morocco. Thanks to the expansion of tourism since the mid-1990s, they've experienced something of a renaissance. See also p117.

Ourika Valley and Oukaïmeden

Restaurants

🍴 Le KM9 (pronounced *'kilomètre-neuf'*), 9 km from Marrakech, as the name suggests, on the Ourika road, **T** 044-376373. *Daily for lunch and 0800 till late. Four set-price menus from 170-290dh.* A sort of country pad-cum- eatery. Very comfy bar with a dining area to the rear. Prize pasta is the order of the day, but there's plenty of other good offerings, too. Unfortunately, unless you spend quite a bit on a taxi (200dh), it's not really viable as an evening out from Marrakech without your own transport. Popular with the *branché* Casablanca weekend set. See also p155.

♯♯ **Auberge Ramuntcho**, at 50 km from RAK, **T** 044-444521, 06-1165182. Best feature of the Ramuntcho's restaurant is the outside terrace. Food variable – clientèle includes numerous tour groups. See also p119.

♯♯ **Dar Piano**, Oulmès, **T** 044-484842, 06-1342884. *Closed Jun-Aug.* See also p119. Good menu at 150dh served in small restaurant – worth a stop if you want something more than a roadside grill. European management.

♯♯ **Le Maquis**, just before the roadside settlement of Oulmès, **T** 044-484531. *Basic menus at 55dh and 120dh.* On the way up to Setti Fatma, Le Maquis makes a reasonable lunch-stop, several levels above your average tajineries. Franco-Moroccan management. See also p119.

Tizi-n-Tichka road (Telouet)

Restaurants

NB If you opt to eat near the village 'square', make sure you know what you'll be paying in advance of ordering.

♯ **Le Lion d'or**, Telouet. In addition to the cheap tajineries in the village, there is now a slightly 'up-market' option near the Kasbah: 60dh gets you salad, tajine and fruit. Numerous stickers testify to the passage of tour groups, and the loos are clean.

Essaouira

Restaurants

ᵞᵞᵞ Riad Bleu Mogador, 23 Rue Bouchetouf, **T** 044-474010. *Daily, lunch and dinner, preferably reserve. Cheapest menu 240dh.* One of the best restaurants in Essaouira. Simple décor and moderately inventive cooking. Three menus with eight offerings from apéritif to desserts. Located off a side-street on your right as you head into the walled town from Bab Marrakech down Rue Mohammed el Gorry.

ᵞᵞᵞ Restaurant de l'Hotel Sofitel-Mogador, Av Mohammed V, **T** 044-479000. On the cheapest menu, at 190dh, there's a choice of three entrées, three main dishes, and desserts. Also a big choice of wines and a comfortable bar to relax in afterwards.

ᵞᵞᵞ-ᵞᵞ Chalet de la Plage, Av Mohammed V, **T** 044-475972. *Daily.* One of the most popular restaurants in town. Provincial bistro feel, sometimes lively of an evening.

ᵞᵞᵞ-ᵞᵞ Chez Sam, in the port, **T** 0044476513. *Daily. Menus at 80dh and 170dh, also à la carte.* One of the oldest restaurants in Essaouira and all very St Malo. Can get quite festive in the evenings. Mediterranean cooking.

ᵞᵞ Les Alizés, under the Hotel Smara at the Skala, **T** 044-4768219. *Daily. Menu 75dh.* All manner of couscous and tajines for which the long dining room is always packed. Worth a visit at least once during a longish stay. Alcohol.

ᵞᵞ Restaurant de l'Hotel du Grand Large, Rue Oum Errabia, just off Rue Mohammed ben Aballah, **T** 044-474880. *Daily.* Serves up a decent, full meal of Moroccan or Italian food, for around 90dh, in a stone-arched room.

♔♔ **Le Mermoz**, Place El Khayma, **T** 044-476485. *Daily 1000-2200. A la carte for around 90dh, menus cheaper.* A tiny place, terrace pleasant during day, upstairs dining room for evenings. Nothing exceptional but centrally located and good for light standard Moroccan restaurant fare.

♔♔ **Pizzeria Le Grand Large**, 2 Rue Oum Errabia, **T** 044-472866. *Daily. Menus from 60-80dh.* Simple, faintly ethnic decor. Nothing outstanding but a warm welcome.

♔♔ **Le Ramsès**, 18 Rue ibn Rochd, opposite the Hotel Cap Sim. Take the street on the left at the town end of Place Moulay Hassan. *Daily, lunch/dinner in summer, dinner (candle-lit) only rest of year. Around 80dh for a full meal.* Has some real Souiri dishes on the menu.

♔♔‑♔ **Il Gabbiano**, 4 Rue Twahouine, off Rue Laâlouj. *Menu at 50dh, but you could eat for more.* Some Italian dishes, cheery, young atmosphere in minimal decoration. Good value.

♔ **Barbecue stands near port-entrance**. *Lunchtime.* A selection of tiny, Jemaâ el Fna-type fish-barbecue restaurants. Waiters race off to the port if the fish runs out. Prices are shown, but make sure you know what you're paying when you order. Popular with day-trippers.

♔ **Café de la Plage**, Av Mohammed V. *Lunch only, daily. Menu at 55dh.* A bit run down, but an institution nevertheless. Just a short walk away from Bab Sebaâ and the port, on the beach.

♔ **No-name restaurant in Souk el Hout**. *Lunchtimes.* A good fried-fish stop in the town, in the central fish-souk, just off the main drag. Address popular with souk workers and locals.

¶ **Océan Vagabond**, Av Mohammed V. *Daily 0900-1800. Breakfast 25dh, sandwiches around 25dh.* On the beach, opposite the islands (think Amazigh surf-bums on an African beach). Pleasant terrace, good place to relax after a windy stroll along the sands. Decent salads.

Cafés and salons de thé

¶¶¶ **Taros Café-Restaurant**, 2 Rue Skala, **T** 044-476407. *Daily 1100-1600 and 1800-2400. Tajines from 65-90dh.* Taros is the name of the ocean wind which rattles and gusts round Essaouira. This Breton-run café-restaurant is a less blustery sort of place, with many a coffee-table book and reading corner. A tad *prétentieux* though.

¶ **Chez Driss**, Rue Hajjali, at the far end of Place Moulay Hassan, (the one inside the walls with all the breakfast cafés). Croissants and fruit juices in the morning.

¶ **Café Fanatic**, Av Mohammed V. *0700-1900. Breakfast at around 15dh.* For surf fanatics. Nice terrace, tiny inside, pool table. Fishermen and young locals.

¶ **Dolce Freddo**, Place Hassan II (the big one near the port, outside the old town). Italian ice-creams. Make sure marauding seagulls don't get the kid's chocolate cornet first.

Safi

Restaurants

¶¶¶ **Restaurant La Trattoria**, aka **Chez Yvette**, Rue Aouinate, an uphill road leading south of the médina, **T** 044-620959. A large Italian restaurant offering a good feed for 200dh, salad and fish main course for 150dh, pizza, lasagne, osso bucco and occasionally tiramisu. A good address if you want don't want to eat in the restaurant of the Hotel Atlantide.

℟-℟ Restaurant Gégène, Rue de la Marine, just off Place de l'Indépendance, **T** 044-463369. Centrally located near the post office and the Château de la Mer, just south of the médina (look out for Wafa Bank). Specializing in fish and Italian dishes, clientèle of regulars, civil servants, people in business and the like.

℟ Restaurant de Safi, 3 Rue de la Marine. Easily identified by bright displays of vegetables and plastic fruit. Roast chicken, brochettes, salads, harira, a few tables outside. Pleasant for a quick feed after a half-day doing the sites of Safi. Parking easy. There are cheaper places at the entrance to the médina, but hygiene there is less reliable.

Oualidia

Restaurants

℟℟ L'Hippocampe, signed as you head down towards the beach, **T** 023-366108. Perhaps the most popular restaurant in Oualidia, part of the well-run Hippocampe (sea horse) hotel complex. Recommended. **NB** 20% VAT will be added to your bill.

℟℟-℟℟ Ostréa II, on your left as you leave Oualidia on the Casablanca road. A branch of the Ostréa restaurant in the port compound at Casablanca. Oyster beds are Oualidia's claim to fame (along with tomatoes), hence this restaurant. Fish and *fruits de mer*, dining on a terrace overlooking the lagoon. Alcohol served. Busy in summer and at weekends. Recommended.

Restaurant A l'Araignée gourmande, Oualidia Plage, near the campsite next to the beach, **T** 023-366144, 023-366447. Seafood with terrace well protected from the ocean breeze. Good service.

Hotel Restaurant l'Initiale, **T** 023-366246. Good Italian menu at 90dh, more expensive menu at 180dh. Candle-lit dining with a warm welcome.

Tomato Beach with its little terrace does seafood, including a plate of fried fish for 40dh and a splendid *tajine de poisson*.

Marrakech's pleasure-city reputation hinges on private *soirées* in médina palaces rather than on raunchy discos. This being a Muslim city, alcohol is not readily available. You can drink in all-male company in small, loud bars in Guéliz or find a smoother, mixed ambience in the bars of big hotels on Avenue de France. There are now a couple of more loungey places in Guéliz, too. However, there is no street with swinging nightlife, as the popular bars and clubs are scattered between the Palmeraie and Guéliz/Hivernage. Clubs are busiest at the weekends when the trendy Casa-Ribatis (dress code: smart-casual) are down to have fun, and during the winter break. Summer is also a busy time. Things get going towards midnight with Euro-house and electro, but it's the Oriental old favourites that really get the crowd going.

Finally, although the médina is in principle dry, apéritifs at sundown on the terrace of a riad restaurant are often possible. Alcohol of all sorts is available in shops in or near the Guéliz food market and some deliver to riads for a small extra charge. During Ramadan, alcohol is sold solely to foreigners.

The emphasis in Marrakech's clubs is on dancing rather than drinking. When the Oriental-fusion-pop kicks in, then the crowd gets going. The Marrakech's annual folklore festival is under new management, so big-name acts may be brought in. Music lovers should try to coincide with the annual Gnaoua Festival in Essaouira, which features international stars. Club entrance is between 100dh and 200dh, depending on whether there is a special night. In most clubs, it's standard practice to reserve a table for your party by buying a bottle or two. There are plentiful taxis to get you home.

Guéliz and Hivernage

Bars

Charly's Cabana, 39 Blvd Zerktouni, opposite the Cinéma Le Colisée, **T** 044-430617. *1200-1430 and 1900-1200. Map 4, C2, p254* More of a relaxed restaurant than a bar with a small courtyard. Aperitifs at 40dh and wine by the bottle at 90dh. For something to eat before a film or after a session at one of the cyber cafés in the neighbouring Ghandouri Complex. The lighting can be a bit bright.

Le Chesterfield, Hotel Nassim, 115 Av Mohammed V. *Lunchtimes until 2300. Map 4, C3, 254* Access via the small shopping centre of the *Hotel Nassim*, a couple of mins' walk from Place Abd el Moumen. Aperitifs around 35dh, beers 20-40dh, whiskies around 55dh. Wooden panelling and armchairs transport you to an English club as imagined by a Marrakchi decorator. Drinks outside next to tiny pool as well.

Le Comptoir Paris-Marrakech, Av Ech Chouhada, almost opposite the *Hotel Impérial Borj*, **T** 044-437702, www.ilove-marrakech.com/lecomptoir. *Map 4, I7, p255* The Red City's trendiest address? Bar, restaurant and small giftshop in an Moorish-Deco villa. All very 'fusion of cultures' – but at a price. Tapas (25dh and rising) compulsory with any alcoholic drink. Beers start at 40dh, cocktails 70dh. Spectacular Oriental dancers some evenings. If on a short break, definitely worth a look before heading off to your dinner date in the médina.

L'Escale, just off Av Mohammed V, on the turning with the Wafa Bank and a shoeshop, almost opposite the Guéliz market. *Lunchtimes and evenings until 2200. Closed Fridays and during Ramadan. Map 4, D3, p254* The best of Marrakech's *chaâbi populaire* (or working man's bars), the place for beers in blokey company. The room at the back serves excellent brochettes or *coquelet* (baby cockerel) and chips (25dh). An excellent address, lively if there's a match on the TV. Handful of tables on the pavement outside where you can sip a beer.

Le Moucharabieh, Hotel Sheraton, intersection Av de France and Av de la Menara, **T** 044-448998. *Daily 1900-0100. Map 4, L5, p255* Beers start at 45dh, cocktails at 70dh. All the big hotels have piano bars of varying descriptions. This is perhaps the most kitsch with its silvery palm trees, blue lighting and general Egyptian rococo feel.

Le Montecristo, 20 Rue ibn Aïcha, Guéliz. *Things get going around 2300. Map 4, A3, p254* Opened in late 2002, this place could fill the gap between pleasant pizzerias and low-life bars. Three floors, three atmospheres, from *fumoir* to tents on the roof terrace. Dance and drink the night away. Some people suggest it has yet to find its public. Drinks not cheap – whiskies start at 70dh.

La Renaissance, Place Abd el Moumen, **T** 044-447188. *1200-2200. Map 4, B2, p254* Diametrically opposite the *Café des Négociants* (good for breakfast). The *mirador* of the neighbouring Hotel Tachfine. A Marrakech favourite for a beer with the best view of Guéliz. Some would say that this is the secular equivalent of the Koutoubia. Both downstairs café (no alcohol) and top floor panoramic bar were closed for a major refit in summer 1993. Pay for your first drink at the counter in the café downstairs and then take the lift to the top-floor terrace. A popular address for a quiet afternoon beer with a view.

Saffran et Canelle, 40 Av Hassan II, **T** 044-435969. *Daily from lunchtime until at least 0100. Map 4, E3, p254* A trendy, pre-club sort of place. The bar-restaurant *La Hacienda* attracts the Marrakchi 30-somethings. Things really get going in the popular karaoke section. In fact, no real need to move on to a club if you get settled in here.

Clubs

Le Diamant Noir, Av Mohammed V. *On a side street on your left as you head down from Rond-point Abd el Moumen. Entry 80dh (week-nights) and 100dh at the weekend. Map 4, E7, p254* A Marrakech favourite, popular with visitors and locals alike. All varieties of funsters and predators shake their booty here to house hits and Oriental. Here are rich kids, foreigners on a business trips and girls with a commercial laugh, Casa-gays (at weekends) and nice girls, expats and local lads on the make. Its handy features include balconies to observe the dance floor and the pizzeria just next to the entrance. Close to Guéliz hotels. Best if you're in a small group, the club follows the French 'buy a bottle, get a table' model.

Paradise, the nightclub of the Hotel Kempinski Mansour Eddahbi, entrance to left of main entrance of the hotel, just off Av de France. *Entry 150dh, drinks at 80dh. Map 4, I2, p255* The city club for the local *jeunesse dorée* and visitors looking to fling a hoof. Musical mix includes R'n'B and electro, plus Raï and Oriental pop. Much less trade than elsewhere.

Le VIP, the former Stars' House, down the street from Le Diamant Noir, and just off the Place de la Liberté roundabout. *Map 4, F7, p254* Had a reputation for boozy punch-ups and sex-workers. Now under new management. A challenger to Le Diamant Noir as queen of the Red City's night.

Al'anbar, on the street behind the Préfecture and Town Hall, **T** 044-380763. *Map 3, A2, p252* Marrakech's latest glitzy offering in the sub-Buddha bar mode. The premises are cavernous, the music deafening, the decor over the top and beyond. Same management as *Chez Ali*, the gaudy fantasia people. No alcohol (yet). You have been warned.

Médina

Bars

Le Churchill, Hotel de la Mamounia, Bab Jedid, **T** 044-444409. *1700-0100 except Mon. Map 3, F1, p252* Jazz some evenings. Black and white photos of long-vanished jazz heroes on the walls, cigars and leather armchairs atmosphere. Clientèle mainly hotel residents.

Riad Tamsna, 23 Derb Zanka Daika, Riad Zitoun el Jedid, **T** 044-385272. *Map 3, E8, p253* Drinks with tapas on the roof-terrace. A must for apéritifs. Also functions as a restaurant (light Lebano-Moroccan cuisine). All in the best possible taste, decorated in sandy greys, bordeaux and deep, woody browns. Boutique has everything for bathroom and bedroom.

Grand-Hotel Tazi, intersection Rue Bab Agnaou ('Le Prince') and Av el Mouahidine. *Map 3, F6, p252* The hotel has little to recommend it. The bar, however, is one of the few places in the médina for a cheap drink (beers at 25dh). Fairly popular with locals, also tourists from the cheap hotels in the area unwilling to trek up to Guéliz.

Palmeraie

Clubs

New Feeling, Palmeraie Golf Palace. *Entry at 150dh, things get going around midnight.* Access in own car or by grand taxi (can be costly). Spacious and rather smoother than the handful of clubs in the city. Mixed crowd of Moroccans down from Casa, foreign residents and visitors. Lacks the manic feel of the Diamant Noir, but worth a night out nevertheless.

Ourika Valley

Clubs

Le Km 9, (pronounced *'kilomètre neuf'*) on the Ourika road, **T** 044-376373. *Wed-Mon 1930-0100.* Tapas and drinks in loungeish atmosphere with palms. Restaurant serves salmon ravioli and *gratin d'aubergine*, and is therefore popular with visitors tired of tajine. Dance floor gets lively at weekends. However, without your own car, you'll have to hire a grand taxi and get the driver to wait – a potentially costly exercise, given that the ride there and back will be at least 200dh.

Check out...

WWW...

100 travel guides, 100s of destinations, 5 continents
and 1 Footprint...

www.footprintbooks.com

In all honesty, arts events are a bit thin on the ground in Marrakech. The city's dreamy fashionistas entertain at home, and a high percentage of the population is far too close to the breadline to be thinking about cultural events. However, there are hints of change. In addition to the annual film-fest, the city now has a major theatre – chiefly used for comedies in Moroccan Arabic. The Institut français has a small open-air amphitheatre, and austerely restored private palaces host literary events and the odd cultural happening. Otherwise, it's a stroll round 'la Place' to see what the musicians are up to. However, for a change from Jemaâ el Fna's manic troubadors and their rasta colours, there is the razzamatazz option of the sound and light show at the Menara Gardens or even a full kischo-Arabian Nights experience *Chez Ali*.

This aside, it remains frustrating that there is no big venue for local live music. Best get invited to a big wedding if you want to see Moroccans in entertainment mode. And children will of course be delighted by the various goings-on in 'La Place'.

Film

As up-and-coming international destination *à la mode*, Marrakech needed a big annual artistic bash. The autumn film festival was set up to fill the gap – even if the Americans have been loath to show their faces since the occupation of Iraq. Attracting big names from Europe, Africa and Asia, the **FIFM**, to use the Marrakech film-fest's acronym, makes a good counterpoint to the bi-annual festivals in Carthage and Ouagadougou. It helps get North African and Middle Eastern films on the map, as well as giving a lift to Moroccan independent film-makers.

Back in the 1950s, every neighbourhood in Marrakech had its local cinema. A night out at the flicks was quite the thing – the poshest venue was the Colisée in Guéliz, of course, where you could see the latest French and Hollywood movies. While everybody was a fan of Egyptian diva **Oum Kalthoum**'s films, the votes for most popular male star were evenly divided between Egyptian seducer songsters **Abdel Wahhab** and **Farid el Atrach**. With television, the audience changed. Cinemas turned oriental, showing Bollywood epics and kung-fu. Although Moroccan directors began to make films in the 1970s, they never really went mainstream – partly due to censorship. It was years before **Souheil ben Barka**'s groundbreaking *La Guerre du pétrole n'aura pas lieu* (The Oil War Will Not Take Place) could be shown, a critique of corruption and local mores. In the 1990s some distributors and cinema owners began to believe that a locally made film could make them some money. However, even today, it's easier to see Moroccan independent films in Paris than in Marrakech.

Right from its beginnings in the 1970s, Moroccan independent cinema has focused on social issues. 1993 saw the first major commercial success, *A la recherche du mari de ma femme* (*Looking for my Wife's Husband*) by director **Mohammed Abderrahman Tazi**. Set in the old city of Fès, the film tells the tale of a corpulent polygamous jeweller. His comfortable family life turns pear-shaped when problems arise with attractive wife number three. The film with the biggest impact in recent years is undoubtedly **Nabil Ayyouch**'s *Ali Zaoua* (2000) a brutal and poetic tale of three Casablanca street urchins. Interestingly, Ayyouch cut his cinematographic teeth in advertising. Across the board, the tone is freeing up, with films by directors like **Abdelkader Lagtaâ**, **Jilali Ferhati** and **Ferida Belyazid** portraying issues never treated on the stodgy national television. Independent successes at the 2003 FIFM included **Faouzi Bensaïdi**'s *Mille mois* (*A Thousand Months*) and **Narjiss Nejjar**'s *Yeux secs* (*Dry Eyes*).

European and North American directors have often filmed in Morocco. The High Atlas often doubles for the Himalayas (*The Man who would be King*, *Kundun*), while the Atlas Studios at Ouarzazate do a sterling job recreating bits of the ancient Mediterranean (*Gladiator* and a recent Asterix-type *Cléopatre*). Franco-Moroccan stand-up comic **Jemal Debbouze** is planning a studio complex near Marrakech. Back in the 1970s, a whole village near the Red City stood in for Mecca in **Mustapha Akkad**'s *The Message*, a portrait of Islam's early years. Filmed in the best sword-and-sand tradition, the potentially controversial film had the go-ahead from the highest Muslim authorities: in accordance with Islamic tradition, the prophet Mohammed is never shown – although the audience sometimes sees the action through his eyes. The film is now something of a religious artefact. The DVD is out, and copies can be found in all pious homes.

French directors have often set films in Morocco. **André Téchiné**'s 2001 *Loin* is set in Tangiers, portraying the charms and tensions of the 'City of the Straits'. Marrakech is the setting for another piece of social critique, **Jacques Doillon**'s *Raja* (2003), a portrait of riad life from the kitchenside. In the title role is **Najat Bensalem**, a Bab Doukkala girl with no acting experiece but seven years of street life and juvenile detention centre behind her. Her 2003 Mostra prize for best young actress was more than a just reward – more like revenge on life.

PRIX DES PLACES
أثمنة المقاعد ٥ - رقم - ٠٤
BALCON 9.00 بالكون
1er SERIE 7.00 الدرجة الأولى
PRIÈRE DE VERIFIER
الجادم راجعة الصرف قبل
AVANT DE QUITTE LE GUICHE
مغادرة الصندوق
MERCIE
شكرا
LA DIRECTION
الإدارة

Namaste!

Take in a Bollywood epic or spot of Kung Fu at a flea-pit in the médina. Fingers crossed that all the reels arrive on time. The audience gets rowdy when they don't.

Cinema

Cinéma Colisée, Blvd Mohammed Zerktouni, Guéliz, **T** 044-448893. *Mon cheap ticket day, tickets 25dh and 35dh rest of week, no credit cards.* *Map 4, B2, p254* The city's best cinema, comfy and plush – women can see films here unmolested, too. Generally shows Hollywood blockbusters dubbed in French. Occasional art-house offerings by Moroccan and European directors.

Cinéma Mabrouka, Rue Bab Agnaou, Jemaâ el Fna. No phone. *Map 3, E6, p252* The classic rowdy fleapit, heavy with the smell of funny cigarettes. Hindi specials, Hong Kong action and an all male audience.

Institut français, Route de Targa, **T** 044-446930. *Map 1, A1, p248* Your best bet for catching some independent Moroccan cinema. Occasional projections of arty films.

Dance

Contemporary and ballet

The Imazighen of the High Atlas have a strong tradition of what would be labelled 'folk-dancing' in a European context. The **ahidous** and **ahouach** are group dances originally performed during the *moussems*, the annual village get-togethers celebrating a successful harvest. Unless you arrive in a mountain village on the right weekend, your best chance of seeing the Amazigh dances is at the annual **Festival des arts et traditions populaires**, held on July weekends in the Palais Badi.

While many young Marrakchis are not averse to a boogie in the city's various nightclubs, there is no contemporary dance scene to speak of. (If in Casablanca, you might see whether the **Ballet**

Zinoun, the country's only contemporary dance troupe, has anything on. Check the press (*L'Economiste*, *Tel Quel*) for details.)

Music

The Red City likes a tune, as the numerous shops selling pirate CDs are witness to. Tastes are eclectic: among his dusty cassettes, the average Marrakchi taxi driver will have Egyptian classics from the 1950s, something by the grande dame of Lebanese song, **Fairouz**, a spot of Algerian **raï**, and a hit album by Moroccan diva **Samira ben Saïd**. The last year or so has seen Moroccan protest songs of the 1970s back in fashion – the classics by **Nass el Ghiwane** (*Les gens du voyage*), have been reworked. Your average adolescent will be listening to Egyptian pop (try **Amr Diab**), as well as Bob Marley, Janet Jackson and Justin Timberlake. So all in all, there's quite a lot of cultural fusion around. Nevertheless, there are a number of well-defined categories of local music – for more info check **www.maroctunes.com**.

Venues

Where can the visitor have an evening of local music? You'll certainly get some musical accompaniment, generally in the form of a small orchestra, in the plusher restaurants. But in all honesty, there are no live-music venues as such in Marrakech or Essaouira. On 'la Place', you're certain to find a couple of small groups in residence, playing the old *ghiwaniate* to small circles of admirers. And you'll have a brush with a gnaoua or two, twirling their heads to get their cap tassles nicely spinning. But the better local singers are only to be found at private wedding parties. And for those you need an invitation. So it's watch this space until the Red City gets a music festival to complement the cinema bash. However, the region is not a total write-off for music fans. There are at least two music festivals in Essaouira, **Les Alizés** in the spring and the

Festival des Gnaouas in early summer, see p169 and check www.festival-gnaoua.co.ma. And if in Morocco in late May, you could travel up to Fès (8 hours by bus), for the annual **Festival des musiques sacrées** (see www.fezfestival.org).

Andalusian music

Small orchestras are the basis of the high musical tradition in Morocco. This is the sort of music played by white-robed gentlemen in fezzes during banquets. The basic instruments are the violin (*kamanja*), the lute (*el oud*), the flute (*el rbab*), the tambourine (*tar*) and the *darbouka*, a waisted drum. In Moroccan Arabic, this form of music is referred to as *el ala*, in European languages it's called Andalusian music. Accompanying singing can be solo and choral and the lyrics are always highly poetic. To the uneducated ear, *el ala* can be a little monotonous – even soporific. Though the *nouba*-s or songs tend to be long, the rhythm speeds up in the final phases.

Gnaoua

Morocco's best-known musical export, gnaoua, springs from a fusion of Muslim saint cults and African mysticism. While Marrakech and Essaouira are the twin cradles of gnaoua, the name would seem to be a corruption of Guinea, a reference to the African slave origins of the genre's founders. Gnaoua music is based on the gentle clashing of giant metal castanets and an undercurrent of bass thrumming provided by a *guimbri*. It was central to trance rituals in saints' shrines. Further Islamic credentials are provided by spiritual protector Sidna Bilal, a freed black slave and the first Muslim to make the call to prayer. Gnaoua influences are clear in Moroccan protest music (see below) and newer fusion music – see the band **Saha Koyo**, for example.

Dekka marrakchia

Kids running round battering small clay drums? Small boys hurling firecrackers round the street? Drumming and chanting late at night in the derb? Yes, it must be **Achoura**, the tenth day of the Muslim month of Muharram, a feast day whose origins are forgotten but which gives Marrakech a carnival air. The drumming ritual of the dekka, specific to Marrakech, is central to Achoura. A slow mystic rite, all about the criss-crossing of drum rhythms, it is unlikely to come under the tourist gaze – but can certainly be heard from afar.

Moroccan protest song

In 2003, the grand-daddies of Moroccan *chanson engagée*, **Nass el Ghiwane**, celebrated their 33rd birthday on 2M, the country's second TV channel. The five founder members grew up in Hay el Mohammedi, a poor neighbourhood of Casablanca. Their success was based on giving the rhythms of the countryside an urban twist in a time of repression. The group's rise to fame was rapid – their gig at the Olympia, Paris, drew an audience of 400,000. Today, the best known songs – *Al-Sinia*, *Alhal*, *Ya Moullana* – are nationwide classics, and favourites with the itinerant musicians on Jemaâ el Fna, too.

Raï

Popular across North Africa, raï is to Algeria, its home, what tango is to Argentina and fado is to Portugal. Born in the port city of Oran, close to the Moroccan border, raï is a genre on its own, taking traditional Arab tunes, adding an overlay of Hispanic brass while synthy riffs replace the plaintive flute solos. The word 'Raï' translates as 'opinion', but it functions more as a filler, embroidered as a sort of 'tralala' sound. **Cheikha Rmiti** is the grand old lady of raï, **Hasni**, **Khaled** and **Mami** are the big stars. Morocco now has its own brand of raï, mainly from Oujda in the northeast.

Shows

Compensating somewhat for the lack of life music and theatre, Marrakech has a number of **tourist spectacles**. These range from the tacky to the kitsch. The best known – and longest running – is Chez Ali. Adults may find the Disneyfied take on Morocco's heritage tiring. Kids, however, tend to lap up the sound and colour, so worth bearing in mind if you're stuck for something to do.

Chez Ali, beyond the city limits, they pick you up, **T** 044-307730, chezali@wanadoo.net.ma, see also www.ilove-marrakech.com/chezali. Dancers, musicians and acrobats, even a princess and a sultan flying over the assembled tourists on a carpet. What more could one ask of the Orient?

Al Menara son et lumière, Menara Gardens, near Av de France, **T** 044-439580, www.coleurs-marrakech.com/numero3. *Tickets 400dh numbered seating, 250dh other. Accompanied children under 12 free.* Created by a Franco-Moroccan team whose credentials include light shows for the city of Lyon and the opening ceremony of the Hassan II Mosque in Casablanca.

Theatre

Sadly, Marrakech has very little to offer in terms of theatre, apart from one-off visits by European theatre groups to the **Institut français** (see page 162).

Théâtre royal, Théâtre Royal de Marrakech, Av de France, Guéliz, **T** 044-431516. *Map 4, F2, p254* Puts on Moroccan boulevard comedies, on occasion which you'd need very good local Arabic to understand.

Two big annual events draw the crowds to the Marrakech region: the big Gnaoua and world music festival in Essaouira (early June) and the film festival in the Red City (late September). At the Gnaoua event surf groupies and post-hippies get together with ethno-beat enthusiasts and local gentry. Concerts are open-air, the historic ramparts of Essaouira making a fitting backdrop. Marrakech's big cinema-fest, the FIFM, is a ritzier occasion altogether. Stars and starlets, royalty and rogues rub shoulders with the big cinema names from the South. Alongside the round-tables for *cinéastes*, open-air screenings of Bollywood film draw the crowds to Jemaâ el Fna. Marrakech also has a big July folklore festival, traditionally a showcase for Morocco's huge range of traditional music and dance. If new festival management has its way, this event will take on an ethnic character, bringing it in line with the Essaouira Gnaoua bash. More discreetly, Essaouira also has a spring chamber music do. Finally, long-established traditional festivals or *moussems*, generally in late summer, are worth catching, especially as the tradition seems to be disappearing.

April

Printemps musical des Alizés, Essaouira. (Last weekend of April) For more information try www.alizesfestival.com or www.essaouiranetcom. (Updating of the official website is slow.) Essaouira is something of a melomane's town. The Alizés spring music festival focuses on chamber music. Set up by the Association Essaouira-Mogador and royal advisor André Azoulay, the festival is named for the trade winds which blow in from the Atlantic. Events are held in Dar Souiri on the Rue du Caire, just off the Bab Marrakech square, and in the town's Catholic church. Recent guest musicians have included Korean violinist Dong Suk Kang and Palestinian pianist Salem Abboud.

Note that a festival of traditional Moroccan urban music, a '**Festival des Andalousies**' is projected for Essaouira, turning it into the 'town of the three musical festivals'. This fits nicely with a line of official rhetoric which insists on Morocco being a *terre de tolérance*, where each of the three great monotheistic religions have (or have had) their place.

May and June

Festival of the Gnaouas and World Music (Late May/first week of June). For more information: www.festival-gnaoua.co.ma (the site doesn't get early updates for the coming festival, so try also www.essaouiranet.com or www.couleur-maroc.com to get a feel for what might be happening). In Essaouira, the festival office is in Dar Souiri on Rue du Caire.

The word *gnaoua* probably derives from Guinea. At Marrakech and Essaouira, Gnaoua refers to trance-music and dances performed by descendants of freed slaves from West Africa. Essaouira is the gnaoua centre and the musical tradition runs deep in certain local families. In 1998, the Association Essaouira-Mogador and local politico/royal advisor André Azoulay launched the Gnaoua festival. The open-air concerts were free. The 2003 edition of the festival (theme 'transe-atlantique') attracted nearly 200,000 spectators – raï star Cheb Mami played the final concert. Events, still largely free, are held on the esplanade at Bab Marrakech and on Place Moulay Hassan near the port. If you are planning in being in Essaouira for festival week, make sure you book your accommodation well in advance.

July

Festival des arts populaires de Marrakech. Try website: www.ilovemarrakech.com/marrakesh/popularts. In 2004, the Marrakech Festival of Popular Arts will be in its 40th year. This oldest of Morocco's festivals started with spectacular displays of traditional dance and music in the vast precinct of the Badi Palace. However, the June event nearly died a death in the 1990s. Shows got cancelled, the lighting fizzled, the original folklore dance concept had come to seem dated. In 2003, a new team took over. As peak season is now all year in Marrakech, the idea is now to have events on every weekend in July. Alongside the Amazigh dances and Gnaoua musicians, there will be a more concerts in a wider range of settings.

Fête du Trône (30 July). Commemorates Mohammed VI's accession to the throne in 1999. The most important secular public holiday in Morocco. People take a long weekend to get home to see family. Flags and light-bulb garlands are everywhere and there are occasional fireworks. In rural areas local authorities put up tents providing free entertainment on edge of towns. Officials and local figures gather, there may be a *fantasia*, cavalry charges performed in front of the tents, traditionally to show loyalty to the *makhzen* (the royal powers that be). Real pachas do not flinch when muskets are discharged by charging cavalrymen a few metres from the tents.

August

Moussem de Setti Fatma In the villages of the High Atlas, the summer months are marked by a series of *moussems*, long-established traditional celebrations focusing on local saints. These tend to be a mix of agricultural fair and clan gathering with a bit of religious ceremonial thrown in. One of the best known is at Setti Fatma, up the Ourika Valley – nice and cool compared to Marrakech in the summer.

In recent years, the authorities have tried to have moussems cancelled. The reason given is the health risks generated by large numbers of people gathering in camping grounds with poor facilities. Underlying this may be the worry that festivals are a good opportunity for rigourist Muslim groups to spread their word through cassettes and informal sermons. In some cases, village councils have cancelled the moussem, preferring to put the money into local development projects. (In Aremd, near Toubkal, moussem money went into a small water reservoir for the village.) Still, it is sad that a part of Morocco's rural heritage seems to be disappearing.

September/October

Festival international de film de Marrakech (FIFM) For more details see www.festivalmarrakech.com. Try also Morocco's second TV channel's site, www.2m.tv.evasion/festivals. Launched in 2000, the FIFM is now the leading cinema festival in Africa, leaving older, more 'third-worldist' festivals like the FESPACO (Ouagadougou) and the JCC (Tunis) in the shade. Alongside the official selection of 10 films, the FIFM has a special *Mawahib* (talents) section. In 2003, the theme was 'post', as in Post-Apartheid, Post-War, etc. The big prize, the *Etoile d'or*, went to Bosnian director Zijad Mehic for *Au feu*. Most popular of all, however, was the special Bollywood section. Morocco is a big consumer of Hindi films – everyone understands *namaste* in Marrakech.

The festival now seems set for the first weekend in October. Audiences mix Marrakech dignitaries and champagne socialists, palace officials and French arty-types, plus a sprinkling of would-be starlets from Casablanca. Opening and closing events (invitations only) are held in the Badi Palace. Most screenings are in the Cinéma Colisée, Guéliz and the Palais des Congrès, Av de France. Side events may be held in the Institut français, Route de Targa. A giant screen sometimes goes up on Jemaâ el Fna, much to médina residents' delight.

Movable feasts

The population of Morocco is over 99% Muslim and the major Muslim festivals are public holidays. However, as the Muslim calendar follows the lunar cycle, the Muslim or Hegira year is 11 days shorter than the standard international year. Therefore religious holidays are constantly on the move, coming forward by 11 days each year. Main holidays are as follows, with projected dates in brackets (NB The Christian year 2004 corresponds to 1424-1425 in the Hegira calendar).

Dates of main Muslim festivals in 2004 Ras el Am (Muslim New Year) 10 February. Aïd el Mouloud (The Prophet Mohammed's birthday) 3 May. Start of Ramadan 16 October, annual month of fasting, gives a whole new meaning to the term 'break-fast'. No food, no drinking of any kind, no smoking and no love-making during daylight hours. Beware drivers speeding blindly towards their *iftar* meals as sundown approaches. The whole country turns slightly manic. Aïd el Fitr 14 November. End of Ramadan, marked by family visiting. Aïd el Kebir or Aïd el Adha 1 February, two lunar months after the end of Ramadan. Families sacrifice a sheep or goat, commemorating how Allah sent Ibrahim a lamb so he didn't have to sacrifice his son. **NB** Dates are approximate, the final decision depending on sightings of the waning moon.

Shopping

Retail therapy is everywhere in the Red City. (One jaded European resident was heard to remark that there is nothing to do in Marrakech but shop.) The souks are filled with craft items and if the idea of a suffocating summer afternoon in the souks is too much, Guéliz has some very upmarket boutiquey places with air conditioning. Though many items will be familiar (Marrakech also exports crafts by the ton), prices are lower than in Europe and you can get an idea of how much you should expect to pay by visiting the government-run craft centre, the *ensemble artisanal*, on Avenue Mohammed V.

The big plus of shopping in Marrakech – and to a lesser extent, Essaouira – is that there is good stuff for all pockets. You can find very reasonably priced thuya wood boxes and trays, painted wood mirrors, ceramics and *belgha* (leather slippers). Wrought iron mirror frames, for example, are cheap – but a little awkward to pass as hand-luggage. At the top end of the market, there are now a number of purveyors of *haut décor*, most of whom are able to ship back to Europe.

★ **Marrakech shops**

ᗺ
ᴇ
ᴤ
ᴛ

- **Côté Sud**, Av de la Liberté, Guéliz, p182. Good mix of crafts.
- **Ben Rahal**, Av de la Liberté, p181. Small carpet emporium.
- **Riad Tamsna**, Riad Zitoun el Jedid, p178. A selection of upmarket accessories.
- **Chic Caftan**, Rue Mohammed Beqqal, Guéliz, p182. A selection of traditional and elegant Moroccan clothes for men and women.
- **Chez Kabir**, Souk des Grains, Essaouira, p187. Made-to-measure raffia sandals.

Since the early 1990s, **craft production** has taken off in a big way, with a range of new products, notably in metal and ceramic, being added to classic leather and wood items. The influence of the international decorator set can also clearly be felt. Close to the Dar El Pacha, in the Bab Doukkala neighbourhood, are plenty of antique dealers, and in Guéliz, innovative and chic interiors boutiques.

Generally, the best **bargains** are of course to be had in the médina souks and the regional markets held once a week in country villages. Prices in Guéliz are fixed and often more expensive than the médina. However, bear in mind that if you visit a médina shop with an official tourist guide, his commission will be built into what you pay for your purchases. Don't be pushed into buying what you don't want: craftwork overdose can leave you feeling a little dazed and confused. See box on bargaining techniques, next page.

Opening hours are irregular, but as a general rule, places in Guéliz open around 0900 and close for a long lunch break from 1230/1300 to 1430/1500, evening closing being around 1900. In the médina, many smaller shops close all Friday afternoon, from 1130 onwards, and Sundays, too. Big tourist bazaar type places open everyday.

Shopping

Marrakech

Antiques and art

The best antique shops and art galleries are in Guéliz but there are two other concentrations of antique sellers, on the pedestrian Rue Dar el Bacha (a couple of large antique emporia) and around the Mouassine Mosque (smaller shops with bits of old silver, textiles etc).

Adolfo de Velasco, Hotel La Mamounia, **T** 044-445900. *Map 3, F1, p252* The ageless Adolfo, he of the wafting caftan and imperial gaze, began his career a while back in Cadiz. He's the man to contact if you're short of an exquisite Indian screen or two. *Haut décor* for the Palmeraie set. (There is a second de Velasco shop in Tangiers.)

Amazonite, 94 Blvd Mansour Eddahbi, Guéliz, **T** 044-449926. *Mon-Sat 0930-1300 and 1500-1930. Map 4, D3, p254* Almost opposite the Odissea Italian restaurant. A long-established address, much visited by small, upmarket tour groups. Best buys: old silver, Moroccan ceramics, bibelots of various kinds. Expensive.

Bab Fteuh, a push and a shove away from the Café Argana. *Map 3, D7, p252* In among the shop fronts selling plastic household goods and clothes, look out for the entrances to a couple of *fondouks* (former merchants' quarters), now specializing in old stuff. (The entrance to the bigger one is practically next to the only plant stall). Metalwork, green ceramics from Tamegroute, bits of camel litters, bedouin camping equipment. Certain nomadic tribes are travelling very light these days. Some very good buys.

Dar Bou Ziane, 20-21 Rue Sidi el Yamani, Leksour, **T** 044-443349. *Map 3, B5, p252* Asiatic, Syrian and Moroccan antiques on premises

Bargaining is expected in a lot of shops and can prove a tedious business, on occasion ending with tantrums on the part of the seller and a line of argument running something along the lines of "you don't want to buy from me because you're a racist" or "you're not my friend any more because you didn't buy from me." You are on holiday, you don't need this, and there are ways to minimize the hassle.

Don't express interest unless you are actually interested. Be polite – but not apologetic. Think – do I really need that ceramic bowl? That little wooden box? The answer? Generally no. But if an item really pleases you, think whether you can afford it and how much it would cost you back at home. Then go for a price which suits your pocket. Voices should on no account be raised – there are more interesting things to do than argue over a 25dh price difference. Remember, the salesman is on home ground, can shout louder and unless you're the souk hound from hell, knows his clientèle and profit margins very well. But also remember that whether you buy or not, he's going to do reasonably well thanks to the underpaid workforce slaving away in some dank workshop. Above all, bargaining for souvenirs is not a life-and-death business, and should not be treated as such.

NB Shops generally have the old-fashioned coupon machines for credit card transactions. Check the price written on the receipt carefully.

which used to be a flour mill. The place to buy your marble fountain or Damascene mother-of-pearl love seat. Everything for the ideal oriental home including wild wrought iron and ram-horn chandeliers by designer Med. But who knows how many kasbahs were pillaged to stock their antique wooden beams section?

Khalid Art Gallery, 14 Rue Dar el Bacha, **T** 044-442410. *Daily 0930-1900. Map 2, H7, p250* Huge range of daggers and doors, ceramics and carpets, jewellery, textiles and even manuscripts.

L'Orientaliste, 15 Rue de la Liberté. *Map 4, C3, p254* Upstairs some of the smaller ceramics and metal items are exclusives (which you might find in a workshop in a corner of the souks). Take a look in the basement for old travel posters, mid-20th-century paintings and semi-antiques. Something for everyone here.

Marco Polo, 55 Blvd Zerktouni, Guéliz, **T** 044-435355, marcopolo@cybernet.net.ma. *0900-1900, closed Sun. Map 4, B2, p254* In the arcade on the same pavement as the Café des Négociants. This is where you go to spend a few thousand euros on an Art Déco bronze, Kashmiri textiles or 400 kg garden urns. Where Nero takes Miss Thing shopping for her new villa in the Palmeraie. Smooth reception.

Matisse Art Gallery, Immeuble Ghandouri, 61 Rue de Yougoslavie, Guéliz, **T** 044-448326. *Mon-Sat 0930-1300 and 1500-1930. Map 4, C2, p254* A handy, pleasant gallery, owned by one Youssef Falaky who can advise on trends in the local art scene. Features contemporary Moroccan artists. Framing service too.

Souk Semmarine, make your way into the médina at the 'entrance' just opposite the Hotel-Résidence de la Place. After some winding you eventually come through an arch into the wide, paved souk. *Map 3, C7, p253* There are some big antique shops and carpet emporia here, some of them very expensive.

Cosmetics and bath products

Riad Tamsna, 23 Derb Zanka Daïka, Riad Zitoun el Jedid, **T** 044-385272, www.tamsna.com. *Map 3, E8, p253* The address for essential oils, soaps, bath-robes and the like. Actually, this address could be listed under clothes, crafts and home furnishings, too. Expensive but worth a look if you have plenty of time.

Rahba Kedima, in the central souk zone. *Map 3, B8, p253* Several small shops where you can pick up traditional bath products for a handful of dirhams. Bath gloves, terracotta scrubbers, incense. They'll fill you a plastic bag of gooey, black, homemade shampoo for your trip to the hammam.

Yves Rocher, 13 Rue de la Liberté, next to L'Orientaliste. *Map 4, C3, p254* For the basic lotions and potions you forgot in the rush. A French franchise popular in Morocco.

Books and newspapers

The French daily press and some English-language newspapers can be found at the kiosks in the vicinity of Rond-Point Abd-el-Moumen, in Guéliz. The biggest kiosk, easily spotted, is next to the tourist office and roughly opposite the Café des Négociants. As for books, despite the presence of the Université Cadi Ayyad, Marrakech is not the most intellectual of towns. Nevertheless, there are a couple of places where you can stock up on large coffee table books, maps and recent Moroccan fiction in French.

Dar Chérifa, 8 Derb Chorfa el Kebir, Mouassine, **T** 044-4426463. *Map 3, B6, p252* Restored building which is home to Marrakech-Riads, who rent quality restored houses. A good place to leaf through some of the numerous coffee table books on Morocco, even if you're not in purchasing mode. Occasional literary events.

Librairie d'Art ACR, 55 Blvd Zerktouni, Guéliz, www.acr-edition.com. *In a small arcade close to the Café des Négociants. Left as you face the café. Map 4, B2, p254* The Moroccan outlet for ACR,

French publisher of expensive art books founded by one M Rafif. Small selection of guides and novels. Worth a look if you have lots of time.

Librairie Chatr, under the arcades at the top end of Av Mohammed V, near the Shell station and the intersection with Rue Abd el-Krim el-Khattabi. *Map 4, B1, p254* The extensive book section, the best in the city, is at the back of the shop, with coffee table books and guidebooks, including Atlas Mountain guides in French on the back wall and novels in English in the far right hand corner. The front part has drawing and office materials and some good postcards. **NB** The bookshop opposite, once a very good second to the Librairie Chatr, is currently closed.

Librairie-Papeterie el Ghazzali, 51 Bab Agnaou, handily next to the *Café Lipton* just off Jemaâ el Fna. *Map 3, D6, p252* North African novels in French, some maps and guide books, also postcards, newspapers and office stuff. Small and a bit frenetic.

Musée de Marrakech, Place Ben Youssef, **T** 044-390911/112. *Map 3, A9, p253* Small bookshop stocking most notably exhibition catalogues and a good selection of reproduction old travel posters and cards. Stamps sometimes available.

Riad Tamsna, 23 Derb Zanka Daika, Riad Zitoun el Jedid, **T** 044-385272, www.tamsna.com. *Map 3, E8, p253* Has an eclectic selection of books and reproductions of old travel posters, worth a look if you've stopped by to have a tapas on the terrace or lunch.

Carpets

Unless you have plenty of floor space to cover, it's a good idea to have a clear idea about what you really want before you start a session in a hot carpet bazaar. Souk Semmarine has some big carpet emporia. Try several to get an idea of the goods and the prices. A good dealer will be able to arrange for shipping of larger items. Be sure to check about customs arrangements at your end.

Ben Rahal, next to Intensité Nomade on Rue de la Liberté, **T** 044-433273. *Map 4, C3, p254* A small, calm shop which allows you to get a good feel for Moroccan carpets. Not the biggest choice, but they have good connections.

Au Minaret de Mouassine, 56 Fhel Chidmi, Mouassine, **T** 044-441357 or **T** 061-181194. *Map 3, B7, p253* Owner Hassan Errijaji is English-speaking and has years of experience.

Clothes and accessories

There are quite a few souvenir shops and shops selling clothes and luggage on Av Mohammed V. There are number of little boutique-type places on Rue de la Liberté, which cuts across Av Mohammed V just after the main food market in Guéliz, on your left as you come up from the médina. Also have a quick trawl along Rue Mohammed Beqqal (turn left just after the restaurant La Taverne, which itself is almost opposite the Cinéma Colisée).

Beldi, 9-11 Souikat Leksour, **T** 044-441076. *Ma p3, C5, p252* Fine selection of traditionally-tailored clothes, mainly for women, for drifting round in at your riad soirée. Waistcoats and flowing shirts for men, too. Expensive. Make sure that this really suits you – do you need an embarrassing embroidered robe in your closet?

Chaussures Ben Youssef, Kaâte Bennahi, 6 Souk Ahl Fès, **T** 044-377810. Small workshop, easily missed, behind the medersa. Go straight on instead of turning left for Dar Belarj, the workshop is on your right. *Map 2, H9, p251* The place to buy the best babouches, prices between 200-280dh, materials used include old flat weaves and modern silks. Beautiful presents. Although the workshop produces mainly to order, there are always a few nice pairs of *belgha* in the window.

Chic Caftan, 100 Rue Mohammed el Beqqal, no 2, **T** 044-435093. *Mon-Sat 0900-1300, 1500-2000. Map 4, C2, p254* Almost opposite the Galerie Bikenmeyer. As the name suggests, elegant women's gear, some men's *gandouras* and *djellabas*. Beautiful babouches with a modern touch. Where the traditional upper-crust of Marrakech buys its Moroccan gear. Prices start at 1,300dh for a caftan and climb steeply. Post-shopping refreshments at the neighbouring Kenzemène *salon de thé*.

Intensité Nomade, corner Av Mohammed V/Rue de la Liberté. *Map 4, C3, p254* Tasteful clothes and leather goods for up-scale people. Quality luggage upstairs, large clothes section for both men and women in the basement.

Place Vendôme, 141 Av Mohammed V. *Almost opposite the food market. Map 4, C3, p254* Forgot your clutch-bag? *Ma kayin mushkil* – no problem, lots of high quality leather options here. After all, Marrakech is the home of *maroquinerie*.

Souk el Kebir, at the end of Souk Semmarine. Beyond an arch, as you leave Souk Semmarine, the street rises slightly. *Map 3, B8, p253* A huge choice of babouches and traditional clothes here. Prices starting at around 40dh for a very cheap pair.

Handicrafts and home-furnishings

Côté Sud, 4 Rue de la Liberté. *As you come from the médina on Av Mohammed V, turn left after Place Vendôme clothes shop; Côté Sud is about 30 m along on right. Map 4, C3, p254* Boutique owned by craft specialist Sabine Hmami-Bastin. Good choice of embroidery,

***Moul'likama*: local mint-man**
Supplying fresh aromatic plants for those famous healthy infusions.

ceramics and small paintings and frames, also perfumes, candles
and incense. Larger items in the basement. Many articles made
especially for the shop.

D'Altro 1, 21 Fhal Chidmi, Mouassine, **T** 044-444289. *Map 3, B7,
p252* Owner Abd el Moumen Mhaidi. Minimalist decorative
thingies. Lamp bases in tadelakt, simple wood picture frames.
Worth a look during a meander through Mouassine.

La Maison de Bali, 65 Av Mohammed V, opposite the food
market, **T** 044-436312, maisondebali.com. *Map 4, C3, p254*
Second shop in Immeuble Ghandouri. Accessories, textiles and
lighting in the Av Mohammed V shop, imported teak furniture in
the Ghandouri arcade. Give your *riad* an Indonesian feel.

Mohammed Ahmouchi, 48 Place Ben Youssef, near the Musée de Marrakech. *Map 3, A8, p253* High quality hand-painted frames and boxes, tables and lattice-work.

Place des Ferblantiers, aka **Batha el Qzadriya**, near the Palais Badi' and Bab Berrima, the metal-workers' souk. *Map 3, H8, p253* The place to look for those metal garden accessories which were (no doubt) all the rage two summers ago. Items as sold in ethnic déco shops at home, but at a fifth the price. Enjoy the smell and hiss of the forges.

Scènes de lin, 70 Rue de la Liberté, **T** 044-436108. *Almost opposite the Hotel du Pacha. Mon-Sat 0930 to 1230 and 1430-1930. Map 4, B4, p254* Rather nice *linge de maison*, as they say at *Marie Claire* magazine. Tablecloths, cushions, bedspreads, all very beige. Discreet embroidery to order.

Souk el Khémis, near Bab el Khémis, away from the main sites at the northern end of the médina. *Map 2, D10, p251* The Marrakech junk market. You may be lucky and pick up old Hotel Mamounia key fobs or some relic of the Protectorate days. Moving away from junk these days, but worth a look. Have a bowl of *bssara* (pea and chick-pea broth). **NB** Watch your pockets.

Jewellery

Micheline Perrin, Hotel La Mamounia, **T** 044-388600. *Daily 1000-1300 and 1600-2000. Map 3, F1, p252* All items unique, created by recycling beads and silver from old Amazigh jewellery. Find the perfect necklace here.

Trésorie du Sud, Rue el Mouassine, **T** 044-440439. *Map 3, B7, p253* Perhaps the most interesting of the small jewellers near the Mouassine Mosque.

Rural markets

A look in at a country market can easily be fitted in with an trip out of Marrakech. Such markets serve local needs, although there are inevitably a number of persistent trinket pushers. Men from the mountain villages come down on mule, bicycle and pick-up truck to stock up on tea and sugar, candles and cigarettes, agricultural produce, maybe have a haircut or a tooth pulled. This is the place to sell a sheep, discuss emigration or a land sale. There may also be some Islamic purists peddling cassettes of sermons, perfumes and religious texts. It really hits home at such markets just how different living standards are in the countryside. The markets are dusty, rough and ready sorts of places, and people are paying with the tiny brass coins you hardly ever see in the city. You really get a sense of the fact that people are living from the land and how hard drought can hit them.

Market days Ourika (Mon), Amizmiz (Tue), Tahanaoute (Tue), Ouirgane (Thu), Setti Fatma (Thu), Asni (Sat) and Chichaoua (Sun).

Sports gear

Olympia, Résidence el Mourad, Blvd Mohammed V, **T** 044-439494. Almost opposite the ERAC building (which is on the intersection with the PTT). *Mon-Sat 0830-1230 and 1500-2000. Map 4, E6, p254* Everything for the *sportif*. Tennis rackets and ballet shoes, golf stuff and bicycles. Also rents sports equipment.

Wines and food

The fresh food market in Guéliz is worth a quick look to see what the prosperous Moroccan family is putting in its shopping basket. Most European packaged foods are available in Morocco – at a price – in some form or other. Try the city's *Marjane* hypermarket.

Alcohol is not as universally available as in Europe. Note that the smaller addresses often close on Fridays for sale of alcohol and that during Ramadan, they may close for the duration of the holy month. If you're just over for a few days, then stock up at the duty-free before getting to Morocco, thus avoiding a trip up to Guéliz. Although beer and wine are cheap, spirits are generally more expensive than in northern Europe.

Achkid, coming from the médina, turn left at the *Wafa Bank* on Av Mohammed V; shop is on your left about 30 m on after the junction. *Map 4, D3, p254* The best known stock-everything shop in Guéliz. (*Achkid* is Tachelhit for 'come along'.)

Hassan Oumlile, shop 19 in the central food market in Guéliz, in the middle, on your right as you go through the main entrance. *(0800-1400, 1600-late, Fri and Sun 0800-1400). Map 4, C3, p254* Has a good range of booze. More importantly, they will deliver wine to riads in the médina. Telephone your order on **T** 044- 433386.

Entrepot Alimentaire, a couple of doors left of the *Hotel Nessim* on Av Mohammed V. *Map 4, C3, p254* An excellent selection of imported wines and alcohols. (**NB** Further up the Av Mohammed V, just after the restaurant *Le Petit Poucet*, a good *épicerie* on the corner of Rue Mohammed Beqqal sells wine and beer in addition to all the usual packaged groceries.)

Hypermarché Marjane, on the Casablanca road. Take a *petit taxi*. *Map 1, A2, p248* Vast but rather appalling supermarket stocking just about everything. Importantly, Europeans can buy alcohol here during Ramadan. Towards the end of Ramadan, Moroccans in the carpark will come up to you with cash, asking you to go in for them to buy beers for their first post-holy-month booze-up.

Essaouira and the coast

Art

Galerie d'art Frédéric Daamgard, Av Oqba ibn Nafia'a, Essaouira, **T** 044-784446. *Daily 1000-1300 and 1500-1900*. This is the grandfather of Essaouira's numerous art galleries. Daamgard, Danish by origin, Souiri by adoption, was the first to seek out local talents and promote the local naïve school of painting. Take a look here before browsing round the mini-galleries scattered in odd nooks across the médina.

Clothing

Chez Kabir, aka **Raphia Mogador**, on the central souk des Grains, (the market square on your right off Av de l'Istiqlal as you come from the port), Essaouira, is the ultimate supplier of *babouches* and raffia sandals, which in fact are made from doum-palm fibre. The best are the pointy-toed Aladdin ones. Can be ordered to suit your feet in colours ranging from natural cream to electric green and purple.

Food products

Co-operative Amal, Village de l'Arganier, Tamanar, **T** 044-788141. One of the best places for argan oil. Understand the production process of this most nourishing (and fragile) of oils by visiting this women's cooperative. Sample prices: 20 g bottle of amlou, 40dh, argan oil, 25cl for 80dh.

Essaouira Médina, 8 Rue ibn Rochd, Essaouira. Property rental agency also sells some argan products. If you miss this too, then Casablanca Airport also has a shop selling argan oil after Customs.

Handicrafts

Co-operative Artisanale des Marqueteurs, 6 Rue Khalid ibn Oualid, Essaouira. Wide range of objects in the fragrant thuya wood for which Essaouira is famous: frames and boxes, lamp-bases and chess-boards. Quality uneven. Best boutique? Jawad Baksso.

La Sqala, around the Bastion Nord, Essaouira, you'll find lots of ateliers producing thuya wood items. *Open until about 1930*. Prices reasonable, souvenirs of all shapes and sizes.

Music

Azza Production, 1 Place Chefchaouni, Essaouira. Cassettes at 15dh and CDs between 60dh and 80dh. Focuses on Gnaoua and African music.

Bob Musique, 104 Rue Sidi Mohammed ben Abdallah, Essaouira. Specialists in traditional musical instruments: djembé and darbouka drums, tambourines and and guitars.

Sports gear

No Work Team, 7 bis Rue Houmane el Ftouaki, Essaouira, **T** 044-475272. Just off Rue Mohammed ben Abdallah, almost opposite the *Maison du Sud* does surf clothing and gear. It may be possible to pick up second-hand surf-stuff from departing visitors.

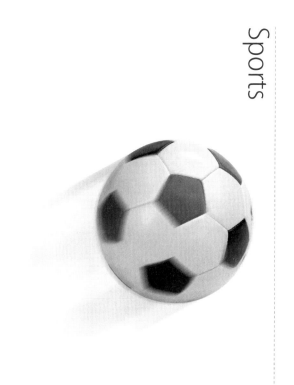

So you thought Marrakech was all oases of cool and fizzing souks? Amazing adventures in the great outdoors are possible, too. Just a couple of hours' drive from Marrakech, the ocean beaches and mountain valleys are attracting the active. Trekkers take to the valleys and plateaux of the High Atlas while surf-sport enthusiasts head for Essaouira. Skiing is possible in Oukaïmeden, birdwatchers will find unique species on the Atlantic coast, golfers have three courses to chose from in the Marrakech palm groves and most big hotels have spas.

The big Marrakchi spectator sport is *koura* (football), and there are two *bahja* (teams) in the national league. Local lads hone their skills in the médina's streets and on stony 'pitches' outside the ramparts. Both national and European league matches are watched in the city's blokier cafés. However, given Morocco's poor performance in World Cups, the Olympic successes of the country's long-distance runners are a much greater source of pride. Athletes like Saïd Aouita, Nawwal Moutawakil and Hichem Guerrouj enjoy star status – and the upcoming generation gets plenty of state support.

Marrakech

Ballooning

Ciel d'Afrique, **T** 044-303135, www.aumaroc.com/cieldafrique. This small Marrakech-based company runs hot-air balloon flights almost anywhere in the country – at a price. The basic excursion involves leaving Marrakech very early for a flight over the Jebilet, the hills north of Marrakech. Four-wheel drive necessary to get to take-off point. Only an option from Oct to May when the balloon can ride on the thermals. Prices around 2,000dh for 1 hr. You can't fly over Marrakech, but will get some good views of the surrounding area.

Football

Kawkab (KACM) football club of Marrakech, one of the best in Morocco, can be seen at the Stade al Harti, Rue Moulay El Hassan, Hivernage. The crowd is lively, scan local press for upcoming matches in Marrakech. *Kawkab* means 'planet'. The number two team is the *Nejma* ('star').

Go-karting and quad-biking

Atlas Karting, Route de Safi, **T** 06-4190537. *Reservation office open 0900-2000. Go-karting 250dh per 30 mins.* Go-kart training courses. Also available quad-biking in the Palmeraie, 2 hrs 30mins, (of which 30 mins intro) 500dh. 340dh extra for a passenger.

Mega-Quad Marrakech, Tamesloht, Km 6 Route d'Amizmiz, **T** 044-383191, www.quadmaroc.com. *Reservations office open 0830-1000 and 1700-2100.* Semi-automatic quads suitable for beginners. Around 15 quads available so small groups possible –

used by the Club Med. Half-day 800dh, easy full day 1,500dh, difficult full day 2,000dh. Prices include transfer from hotel to pistes. Can set up six-day excursions with bivouacs. **NB** Quads take two people.

Golf

Golf was adopted by Morocco's sultans in the late 19th century and the late King Hassan II reportedly made big decisions whilst on the links. Major competitions such as the Trophée Hassan II attract international attention and much local TV coverage. The High Atlas forms a backdrop to the three Marrakech courses. All are open to the public though evidence of handicap is required. October to May is the best period – summer is too hot. From the UK, try: **Exclusive Golf Tours**, **T** 0870-8704700, www.exclusivegolf.co.uk, for packages to Marrakech. See also www.morocco.golf.co.uk.

Marrakech Royal Golf Club, BP 634, Ancienne Route de Ouarzazate, **T** 044-444341. *18 holes, 6,200 m, par 72, round at 400dh.* A beautiful course with lots of shade trees, created in the 1920s by the Pasha of Marrakech and frequently renovated since. Winston Churchill played here.

Club de la Palmeraie Golf Palace, Marrakech, Les Jardins de la Palmeraie, PB 1488, **T** 044-301010. *18 holes, 6,214 m, par 72.* Opened 1993, designed by Robert Trent Jones Snr, this course has thousands of palm trees, seven lakes, and Mauresque-style clubhouse. Cost of round, 550dh.

Golf d'Amelkis, Marrakech, **T** 044-404414. *18 holes 6,657m, par 72, a round costs around 500dh.* The newest of the Red City's courses, said to be one of the most striking in Morocco, designed by CB Robinson, set with palm groves and water traps. Located close to the Amanjena Resort.

Hammams

As the middle classes move out of the médina of Marrakech, the hammams, once upon a time the place where everyone went to have a big wash, seem to get scruffier. On the plus side, certain hotels have hammams. Part of the charm, however, was that the hammam was traditionally a very democratic place where you would find people from all walks of life. Many riads have hammams but they are generally too small to be of much interest. In public hammams, Thursday and Sunday evenings are the busiest times.

Hammam du Pacha, Rue Fatema Zohra, Dar el Bacha. *Men 0400-1200 and 1930 to around 2130, sometimes later; women 1230-1730. Entry 10dh, massage and soapy scrub, 40dh (roughly – at your discretion, really). Map 3, B4, p252* The biggest and most luxurious hammam in the city. Early 20th-century building, identified by big dome. Lie on the hot marble in the innermost chamber to get a good sweat going.

Hammam Ben Youssef, coming from the souks, on your left just before you get to the main entrance of the Musée de Marrakech on your right. Easy to find. *Women in afternoons. Map 3, A8, p253* Clean but used by poorer locals.

Hammams near Jemaâ el Fna. There are a fair number of hammams near 'la Place'. Try **Hammam Riad Zitoun el Kedim**. *Open all day, separate sections for men and women. Entry 6dh, massage 30dh. Map 1, A6, p248* Avoid the Bain Polo.

Hammam Es Salama aka **Hammam Majorelle**, near the wholesale market and the Jardin Majorelle. *Men's and women's sections, entry 6dh. Open 0600-2200. Map 1, A6, p248* Clean, modern.

▶ Pleasures of the bath

Even now, the *hammam*, the traditional bath-house is central to Marrakchi life. Although riads may have a small hammam, you could do worse than take a trip to your neighbourhood scrubbery.

Many hammams come in pairs, with doors to the men's and women's sections side by side. Otherwise, men typically get the morning and evening shifts, women the afternoons from, say, 1400 to 1900.

A hammam usually consists of a changing area, with wooden benches round the wall, where the owner presides. Behind a heavy wooden door is the first of three vaulted wash-rooms. In the innermost (and hottest) chamber, you typically stretch out on the marble floor, heated from below, or make a few vaguely athletic stretching movements to get yourself transpiring. Once the sweat is drizzling, you head for one of the earlier, cooler chambers where people will be energetically scrubbing themselves with rough nylon mittens. Find yourself a space and then, equipped with two or three buckets of water at different temperatures, get washing. You may even go for a massage, which can be horribly joint-stretching, on the men's side. A scrub and soapy washdown is a *gommage*.

A few tips. Bring a couple of towels. Shampoo and fluorescent pink or green scrub-mittens are usually available. Men wear shorts or undies, women just knickers. In the better hammams, you pay after your bath – and get a free glass of tea.

Best times to go hammaming vary. Thursday evening and Sundays see heavy trade, while on weekday nights sports teams come along after training. Avoid hammams near Rue Bab Agnaou, as they see too much tourist trade.

The following small hotels and guest-villas have chic **private hammams** which are sometimes open to non-residents by special arrangement.

Kasbah Agafay, Route de Guermessa, **T** 044-420960.

Les Deux Tours, Douar Abiad, Circuit de la Palmeraie, **T** 044-329525, www.deux-tours.com.

Hunting

Chassamir, 65 Av Mohammed V, Guéliz, not far from Chez Jack'line, **T** 044-449787. Long established agency. Can set up shooting for partridge (Oct to end Dec) and quail (Oct to end Jan). Also wild boar hunting.

Spas

Tikida Garden, Centre de Balnéothérapie (spa), Circuit de la Palmeraie, **T** 044-329595, www.marrakech-tikida.com. Spacious spa with qualified team on hand.

Palmeraie Golf Palace, Circuit de la Palmeraie, **T** 044-301010, **F** 044-305050 (reservations), www.pgp.co.ma. The 'PGP' complex features a spa with sauna, jacuzzi, steam room and various treatments.

Riding

A number of international operators run riding holidays which will start in Marrakech and then involve short road transfers to wilder parts of the Atlas. See for example **www.equine-world.co.uk** or **www.ridingtours.com**.

Club Equestre de la Palmeraie Golf Palace, Circuit de la Palmeraie, **T** 044-301010, **F** 044-305050 (reservations), www.pgp.co.ma. The most suitable stables for children. French management, ponies. Around 150dh/hour.

Club équestre de la Palmeraie, **T** 044-329451, also located in the palm groves.

Swimming

Piscine de la Koutoubia, Rue Abou el Abbes, near the Koutoubia Mosque. *Open summer only.* *Map 3, C2, p252* The municipal pool here was refurbished in 2002. It gets crowded and the water gets a little mucky at the end of the season. Not really for women.

The large hotels such as the **Sheraton**, **Tichka** and **Méridien-Nfis** have pools (although they are not always heated), which can be used by non-residents for a small fee. Outside Marrakech, the multiple pools of the **Palmeraie Golf Palace** are open to non-residents for 150dh.

Tennis and squash

Royal Tennis Club de Marrakech, Rue Oued el Makhazine, Jenane el Harti, **T** 044-431902. *Daily 0700-2200. 100dh/hour.* *Map 4, F5, p254* Has 8 courts (4 floodlit), a club-house with restaurant and a small pool. This is a club, so they may require you to take out membership for a small fee. Lessons with good coaches are available in the evenings.

Palmeraie Golf Palace, Circuit de la Palmeraie, **T** 044-301010. Also has courts but is not very central.

Atlantic coast

Camel trekking

Auberge de la Plage, Club Equestre, Essaouira, **T** 044-476600, aubplage@iam.net.ma. Camel trekking took off in the 1990s with beasts imported from Mali. Treks take you through magnificent scenery along the Atlantic coast.

Cap Sim Trekking, Douar Ghazoua, 8 km south of Essaouira on the Agadir road, **T** 062-201898, www.essaouira.fr. Can provide advice on various outdoor activities in addition to camel trekking.

La Maison du Chameau, Km 7 route de Marrakech, Essaouira, **T** 044- 783254. Around 120dh an hour for an initiation into the mysteries of dromedary riding.

Hammams

Hammam, Rue Abdelaziz el Fechtal, Essaouira. *0600-2300 (men only). Entry 7dh, massage 30dh.* Tiny traditional hammam.

Hammam Mounia Café, 17 Rue Oum Errabia, Essaouira, **T** 06-6014623. *Open daily 0730-0930, 1230-1600, 2000-2230 (men), 0930-1230 and 1600-2000 (women). Entry 50dh.* Body shop aesthetics meet the traditional Moroccan hammam. Café upstairs to recover after your steam and massage.

Riding

Les Cavaliers d'Essaouira, Km 14 route de Marrakech, **T** 065-074889. *100dh per hr, 160dh per 2 hrs, 400dh per day.* Can organize riding through the argan plantations and longer treks with bivouacs.

Spas

Thalasso de l'Hotel Sofitel, Av Mohammed V, Essaouira, **T** 044-479000. The only real sea-water spa in the region, part of the recent (2000) Sofitel, part of the Accor chain.

Swimming

Bathers should be aware of the strong currents on the **Atlantic beaches**. (This explains why Moroccans all seem to stand next to the water rather than go very far in). On many beaches, bathing is prohibited outside the summer season when a coastguard is present. Even he won't be able to do very much should you get out of your depth. At Essaouira, non-residents may use the **Hotel Sofitel Mogador**'s pool for a small fee.

Wave sports

Essaouira has surfing and windsurfing facilities. The surfers are around in the winter months, while from April to October the alizé winds bring the windsurfers in. A few kilometres south, Sidi Kaouki is popular with windsurfers due to persistently strong winds. To the north of Essaouira, Oualidia is ideal for beginners. Try www.purevacations.co.uk for a week's surf-schooling.

L'Océan Vagabond, on Essaouira beach, **T** 061-103777, oceanvagabond@hotmail.com. Qualified instruction in windsurfing, surfing and kite-surfing. Recent equipment. Can put you in touch with surf equipment repairers.

Gypsy Surfer, 14 Rue de Tetouan, Essaouira, **T** 061-947092. Surf clothes and equipment.

No-Work Team, 7 bis Rue Houman-el-Fetouaki, **T** 044-475272. Surf clothing.

High Atlas of Toubkal

Off-road biking

The minor roads and tracks of the High Atlas can provide a good biking holiday. Best times are spring and autumn. There's spectacular scenery, low accommodation and food costs and also plenty of places to bivouac. On the down side, beware of random driving of 4WD vehicles and Mercedes taxis, wild dogs lurking near villages and crowds of kids in poor villages, eager to have a look at everything you have in your numerous paniers.

Rough Tracks, **T** 07000-560749, www.roughtracks.com. UK-based cycling holiday operator with back-up in the Atlas.

Skiing

The best site is 76 km from Marrakech at **Oukaïmeden**. Unfortunately, decreasing snowfall over the last decade or so has got the better of Morocco's reputation as a ski destination. The snow tends to melt during the day, refreezing at night, giving the runs an ice surface.

Exodus, **T** 020-86755550, www.exodus.co.uk. Runs ski-trekking holidays in the High Atlas.

Hotel Kenzi Louka, Oukaïmeden, **T** 044-319080. In addition to quality accommodation can provide info on hire of ski equipment.

Trekking

The western High Atlas, centring on Jebel Toubkal, is now a well-established trek destination for European travellers. You can either set up a trek with one of the agencies (Exodus, Explore or Sherpa, for example) or sort things out when in Marrakech via a local guide who can be contacted via the **Hotel Ali**, Arset el Bilk, Marrakech. Qualified guides will have had proper training from the CFMM up at Tabant, Aït Bougmez. Otherwise, contact one of the local trek companies listed below. Accommodation on a trek will be homely, generally in local homes or bunk houses (*gîtes d'étape*), with a few nights' bivouac too. Rucksacks are generally portered by mules. Best times of year are April to June and the autumn. Note that flash floods can be a problem in the valleys in late summer. Highest peaks are snow-covered in winter.

Atlas Sahara Trek, 6 bis Rue Houdhoud, Quartier Majorelle, **T** 044-4313901, atlassaharatrek@iam.net.ma (may change soon). One of the best trekking agencies in Marrakech with 20 years' experience. Moroccan-born founder Bernard Fabry knows his deserts well. Also runs upmarket accommodation in the remote Vallée des Aït Bougmez, east of Marrakech.

TTM-Trekking Tour Maroc, 107 Rue Saâd ben Errabia, Issil, **T** 044-4308055. Offers ski trekking in Toubkal from 15 Jan-30 Apr, camel trekking by the Atlantic coast, mountain walking guides, meals and all camping equipment provided.

Pampa Voyage (Maroc), Immeubl Jassim, ground floor, 219 Blvd Mohammed V, Guéliz, **T** 044-431052, www.pampamaroc.com. Professionally managed travel agency with a strong reputation.

Mohammed Nour, **T** 044-302189. Very helpful and good for setting up treks for small groups. English-speaking.

Marrakech has long had something of a sulphurous reputation. The very mention of the Red City may bring tears to the eyes of European gentlemen of a certain generation as they remember dear Mustapha, December 1965. Things have moved along a little since. Mass tourism is arriving – but not the rainbow flag. Despite awareness of 'gay identity' among some young Moroccans thanks to satellite TV and the web, plus an influx of gentrifying A-gays, Marrakech remains a provincial sort of place. Apart from emigrating or moving up to Casablanca, the local gay guy has few options: discreet relationships, probably followed by marriage after 30; or, possibly, total flailing queendom. Winter sun notwithstanding, this is not Miami or Mykonos. It follows that there is nowhere that can really be labelled as gay or lesbian in Marrakech – nor would businesses appreciate the label. Still, the city has masses to satisfy the gay sensibility (as specified by the clichés): boutiquey places stuffed with bijou bits and pieces, guest houses like oriental design shrines and a lot of handsome faces.

The gay visitor to Marrakech should remember that this is a city with a huge social divide. While you may be able to jet in for a weekend for a few hundred euros, this will be six months' budget for an entire family in Bab Doukkala. Twenty-year-olds with looks are thus tempted to make some cash on the side with a bit of informal sex-work. If you look as though you have money, you may have some very charming (and commercial) smiles flashed at you as you sip your *jus d'orange* at the Café des Négociants in Guéliz. The price-tag? For you to negotiate, if this is your thing. In other, one-off encounters, you may find yourself in a situation where you are with someone who has very, very little in material terms. So presents – nice clothes, trainers, a watch, maybe a spot of cash – are appreciated.

If you want to meet bona fide Moroccan gays and lesbians quickly, the easiest way is to get onto one of the international chat-sites. Try www.cybermen.com first (largely Francophone). At any one time, this will have a good 20 to 30 Moroccans connected. The Paris-based www.kelma.org, which functions as a sort of forum for gay people in France's North African and black immigrant community (and their friends) has lots of small adverts.

Marrakech is a very small city, however, and locals may be uncomfortable at meeting in a very obvious public place where members of their family or friends might pass by. One reason for this local reticence regarding chance meetings with foreigners is the watchful eye of the Brigade touristique, originally established to reduce the hassle problem. While hassle has been brought under control, the Brigade can still run in a Marrakchi who might just be bothering a foreigner – and extract some blue 200dh notes for release. Some locals, to avoid this problem, register themselves with the police as friends of Mr X, living at Y in Marrakech and carry an official certificate to prove this.

So is sex between men illegal? Yes, although this doesn't seem to stop anyone and to the author's knowledge there have been no cases of Moroccans being brought to trial for same-sex activity in recent years. (Compare with Egypt and the full-scale persecution of local gays during the Queen Boat trials.) If you proposition someone in a flirtatious way, they won't go running off to the police (or their therapist). A 'no thanks, mate' approach is taken.

So, on the whole, the Marrakchis are a tolerant lot. The reptilian Euro-gay prowling Jemaâ el Fna is a well-attested feature of local life and party-goers teetering along the alleys of the médina, shedding sequins in the dust as they head for some luscious riad or other add a spark of glamour to everyday life.

Happily, for the moment, AIDS (*le Sida* in French) is not the huge problem in Morocco that it is in sub-Saharan Africa. Educated Moroccans are more or less well informed about risks thanks to the Francophone media. The country also has a highly active NGO, the ALCS (Association de lutte contre le sida, www.alcsmaroc.org), which has done sterling service to bring the issue to the authorities' and the public's attention. (**NB** While condoms are readily available in pharmacies, water-based gel is not.)

Given the huge inequalities that women face in terms of personal status legislation (divorce, inheritance) and the amount of uphill campaigning still to be done to improve things, it is not surprising that lesbian issues are absent from public life. There have been no cases of Moroccan women being brought to trial for lesbian activity.

Finally, a few words on slang: *branché*, the French for 'trendy', can mean gay in the Moroccan context. The passive partner is an *attay*, 'the giver'.

Listings

At present, there are no accommodation addresses which can be listed as specifically gay here. (Two upscale guest-houses listed in French guides in 2002 have now closed.) If staying in a riad, note that there is not a lot of privacy in many cases as most rooms will open onto a garden courtyard.

Sweet ginger tea and *slilou*
*A powdery, nutty aphrodisiac paste. Best consumed on the hoof on
Jemaâ el Fna, on your way to an interesting assignation in the derb.*

Accommodation

Résidence el Hamra, 26 Av Mohammed V Guéliz, **T** 044-448423, 044-448285. *Almost opposite a Shell station near the intersection of Av Mohammed V and Abd el Krim el Khattabi. Around 380dh for a double. (41) Map 4, A1, p254* Not an exclusively gay address by any means, but not gay unfriendly either. See p112.

Bars and clubs

Comptoir Paris-Marrakech, Av Chouhada, **T** 044-437702, www.ilove-marrakech.com/lecomptoir. *Map 4, I7, p255* Not a specifically gay bar for tapas amongst candles and incense, and occasional oriental dancing. See p151.

Le Diamant noir, heading for the médina from Guéliz, just off Av Mohammed V on your left before you reach the big Liberté rond point. *Map 4, E7, p254* A Marrakchi classic nightspot. An evening here is more or less compulsory. The crowd: locals and visitors of all persuasions, students, gigolos, would-be models, business types, etc. Galleries for ogling the *piste*, comfy settees and corners. Things get going about midnight. Mox levels higher at the weekend when the Casaouis are down for a good time. See also p153.

Hammams

Long gone are the days when Bill W. and various others would disport themselves with footballers at the **Bain Polo**. Just off Le Prince, this is now the backpackers' hammam par excellence. **Hammam el Bayyadine**, just off Derb Debbachi, had a scurrilous reputation. Best to consider hammams as places where you might meet someone. Remember, many médina houses lack running hot water, so hammams are important to a lot of people for washing: San Francisco bath house behaviour of an earlier époque is *déplacé*.

Marrakech has lots to fascinate the seven-to-11s. Although there are practically no child-specific attractions, life is going on all around, out in the streets and in the workshops. Lots of questions will get asked: Why's that little girl carrying a tray of bread on her head? How do they write that in Arabic? Why's your glass full of leaves? You may find yourself riding in a carriage or looking into noisy *foundouks* – where some of the 'employees' may be the same age as your kids. Provided they don't get the Pacha's revenge, a trip to Marrakech will be a memorable one for the kids.

For tiny tots, however, Marrakech is trying. Médina streets are not pram-friendly. Riads have unfenced plunge pools and steep staircases. (However, on the plus side, guest houses can generally set up babysitters and cots and allow you access to the kitchen to prepare food. Processed baby food is available in some pharmacies.)

Although restaurants are not kitted out for small children, a huge fuss will be made of them. Whether they'll do more than pick at the food is another thing. Try them with the steamed snails on Jemaâ el Fna.

Foreign children attract lots of kindly attention, which can be a bit of a culture shock for shy kids. The Moroccan affection for children means that doors which would otherwise be closed often open. Particularly in the rural areas, blond kids will a source of fascination to local children and mothers, many of whom would dearly like to communicate. The love of kids is particularly understandable given that life is very hard for many families. Children are still dying at birth and in infancy in the rural areas, due really to a lack of simple health education.

A few precautions to bear in mind when setting up a trip with kids. If hiring a car via an international agency, specify the sort of car-seat you need – and don't be surprised if your requirements get lost somewhere on the way. Kiddie seats are yet to become a must in Morocco. On the health front, make sure the children's vaccinations are up to date. (Polio is still common). Tap water in Marrakech is safe to drink, but there is plenty of bottled water on sale. On busy Jemaâ el Fna and médina streets keep tight hold, as kids from the land of the supermarket won't be used to the hectic traffic. When booking at a big hotel, check if there is a kiddie pool – and whether it is heated if you're travelling in winter. Most pools are not.

Marrakech might be attractive to some kids as it is short on museums and religious monuments. On the other hand, there are plenty of interesting things to fill a day: a carriage (calèche) ride around the ramparts, an evening gawp at the entertainments on Jemaâ el Fna. The Palmeraie Golf Palace hotel complex north of town has bowling, riding stables, tennis courts, and pools. Older children might enjoy a four-wheel drive excursion up into the High Atlas. At Essaouira, there are wood carvers' workshops and camel riding on the beach. Both Essaouira and Safi have busy, working fishing ports. The advantage of staying in a riad can be that the children might be able to see Moroccan food getting prepared first hand.

Marrakech

Souks, north of Jemaâ el Fna. *Map 3, B/C 7/8, p253* The big attractions will be the apothecaries' booths in **Souk Laghzal**, the former wool market and on Rahba Lekdima. Dried chameleons on skewers, boxes of baby tortoises and the odd miserable raptor. 'Mummy, mummy can I have a leopard skin!' you'll hear them cry.

Musée de Marrakech, Quartier Ben Youssef. *Open daily, Mon closed, 0930-1300 and 1500-1830. 10dh. See also p45. Map 3, A9, p253* If the kids only want to do one museum, it should be this one as it will give them a feel for the grandeur of a Marrakchi palace in the late 19th century. The courtyard is spectacular and there are displays of manuscripts and traditional pottery. The big advantage of this museum is that it comes after a wander through the souks and has a small café with clean loos. Those who are tired can wait here while the older ones go off to have a squint at the nearby **Almoravid Koubba** (see p44), the oldest building in Marrakech and the privately owned **Dar Belarj** (see p47), down the street leading to the entrance of the Medersa Ben Youssef – occasional trendy exhibitions.

Medersa Ben Youssef, Quartier Ben Youssef. *Open daily, Mon closed, 0830-1145and 1430-1745. 10dh. See also p46. Map 3, A9, p253* Kids should definitely take a look at this building. Within living memory, it was full of students, hard at work on Islamic law and the religious sciences. Easily included with a visit to the souks and the neighbouring **Musée de Marrakech** (see p45). In the streets near the Medersa are a number of former merchants' hostels or *fondouks*, now used primarily as workshops. Here you can see a workforce (which looks well below the legal employment age) heating, beating and cutting metal into the intricate arabesques required for decorative lanterns and the like.

This little piggy went to market
Stock up on terracotta piglets at a stall on the Ourika road. Atlas Mountain fauna also includes rarely-spotted mouflon and patient mules to carry bags and even tired children on a hike.

The Tanneries, aka **Dar Debbagh**. *See p48.* *Map 2, H12, p251*
Best visited early morning. Either take a taxi to Bab Debbagh or
thread your way through the streets from the Medersa Ben Youssef
(people will volunteer to guide you for a small fee). Not a visit for
very small kids – you don't want to lose one in a pool of gunge. A
truly medieval sight.

Jardin Majorelle. *Take a cab. 0800-1200 and 1400-1700. Entry
20dh. See p60.* *Map 1, A6, p248* Artistically-inclined kids will like
this garden where giant cactus, bamboos and eucalyptus trees
hide a mysterious deep-blue villa. Goldfish to feed as well.

Atlantic coast

Potteries, Safi médina. *See p94.* School-age children will probably
enjoy taking a look at working pottery in the old town of Safi. Best
time to visit is the morning.

Camel rides, on the beach at Essaouira.

High Atlas

Excursions

Walking at Imlil. Located in sight of Jebel Toubkal, Imlil makes a
good day trip. Take packed lunches – there are small shops in the
village which have fizzy drinks, biscuits etc. Stop in at the Kasbah
de Toubkal, walk up to Aremd through the walnut groves – and
back by the road. Another possibility, for riders, is to hire mules to
take you up the valley.

Directory

Airline offices
Royal Air Maroc, Av Mohammed V, Guéliz, **T** 044-436205, (reservations on **T** 044-446444), info@royalairmaroc.co.ma, www.royalairmaroc.com; Aéroport de la Menara, **T** 044-368516/17/18. Hotline for reservations **T** 0900-008000 (2dh a minute). *Open Mon-Fri 0815-1230 and 1530-1930. Sat and some public holidays 0900-1200 and 1500-1800.*

Banks and ATMs
Plentiful banks with ATMs on Av Mohammed V, Guéliz and Rue Bab Agnaou. **NB** They can run out of money at weekends and during public holidays. **Wafa Bank**, green and yellow livery, most reliable. Queues can be long on Friday evenings, too. Maximum withdrawal is 2,000dh on some machines. Some shops in the souks will exchange euros or even take payment in euros. Banking hours 0915-1100 and 1430-1630 in winters, Mon-Fri, summer and Ramadan hours shorter, 0815-1400. There are currency exchange guichets at the main banks on Av Mohammed V, Guéliz. The one opposite the Cinéma Colisée stays open longer than the others. Commission on travellers' cheques, 11dh per cheque cashed. **Western Union** at the main post offices. Two cash dispensers and **BMCE** bureau de change at Aéroport de la Menara.

Bicycle hire
See p29.

Car hire
Avis, **T** 044- 431180, 07-0174116 (airport) also **T** 044-432525; and **Budget**, **T** 044-432525 (airport), **T** 044-431180. Local companies include: **Concorde Car**, 154 Av Mohammed V, **T** 044-431116, 044-439973, concordecar@iam.net.ma; **Imzi-Tours**, Imm. Saâda, R de Yougoslavie, Guéliz, **T** 044-433934, imzitours@hotmail.com; **Pampa**, 219 Av Mohammed V, **T** 044-431052.

Credit card lines
American Express, **T** 00973-256834. **Barclaycard**, **T** 0044-1604230230. **Diners Club**, **T** 0044-1252513500. **Visa**, **T** 001-4105819994, 410-5813836.

Cultural institutions
Dar Chérifa, 8 Derb Chorfa-Lekbir, **T** 044-426463, www.marrakech-riads.net. Bijou riad running occasional cultural events. **Institut français**, Route de Targa, next to Lycée Victor Hugo, **T** 044-446930. Films, theatre and a library of books in French. Much visited by expatriate residents. Closed Mon and Aug.

Dentists
Dr Hicham Qabli, 213 Av Mohammed V, **T** 044-438604.

Disabled
Morocco's hotels are not well equipped to cater to the needs of the disabled. There are very few facilities. If you are planning a visit, you may find that one of the larger hotel chains in Marrakech (Sheraton, Méridien) or Essaouira (Sofitel) has a couple of rooms adapted for disabled requirements. The médina is awkward to negotiate with wheels, potholes and narrow, crowded streets compound the difficulties. A reliable tour company with a lot of experience in Morocco will be able to tell you if your needs can be met.

Doctors
Pharmacies (see below) can provide quick medical advice and a list of reliable doctors. For an emergency in Marrakech: call the **SOS-Médecins-Maroc**, **T** 044-404040, the private, doctor-on-call service. A visit to a hotel will cost around 400dh. In Essaouira, **Dr Saïd Haddad**, **T** 044-0476910, near the Wafa Bank on the main street.

Electricity

Most of Morocco uses 220 volt electricity and standard Western European two-pin plugs. Some guest houses in older areas may be on the 110 volt system. If you've forgotten your phone charger, most varieties can be bought cheaply in the Rue de la Koutoubia.

Embassies

All embassies are located in Morocco's political capital, Rabat. Europeans check **www.eudel.com**, the delegation of the European Union's site. Americans look at **www.usembassy-morocco.org.ma**, which also provides useful links. The French consulate is behind high walls between the Koutoubia esplanade and Arset el Bilk park, **T** 044-388200.

Emergency numbers

Police, **T** 19. **Fire** (sapeurs pompiers), **T** 15. **SOS Accidents de la circulation** (traffic accidents), **T** 044-401401. **Polyclinique du Sud**, **T** 044-447810. **SAMU de Marrakech** (medical out-call service), **T** 044-433030. **SOS Médecins**, **T** 044-401402.

Hospitals

Wealthier Moroccans avoid public hospitals where standards are variable. Good private hospitals in Marrakech include: **Polyclinique du Sud**, 2 R de Yougoslavie, Guéliz, **T** 044-447999, also **T** 0800-025025; **Clinique ibn Tofail**, R Abd el Malik, Guéliz, **T** 044- 438718, not to be confused with the neighbouring public hospital of the same name.

Internet/email

Marrakech has a good number of cyber cafés, handily located near cheaper hotels. Prices are around 10dh/hour, although you may find 6dh/hour places, too. In Guéliz: **Immeuble Gandouri**, entrance opposite the Cinéma Colisée. In the médina: **Cyber Koutoubia**, Rue Bab Agnaou; Cyber Kenaria, Riad Zitoun el Jedid.

Language schools

Surprisingly perhaps, Marrakech has no language schools offering Arabic and Tachelhit courses to foreigners. The best institution in Morocco for those wishing to learn Arabic is **ALIF** (Arabic Language Institute in Fès), www.alif-fes.com.

Launderette

Blanchisserie du Sud, R Bab Agnaou. Open 0800-1300 and 1400-2100. 7dh for a shirt or trousers. Will even do sleeping-bags. **Koutoubia Pressing**, close to the Arset el Bilk garden.

Left luggage

The ONCF main rail station in RAK has a *consigne* (left luggage service). Such services may close, given the 16 May 2003 terrorist attacks in Casablanca.

Libraries

Institut français, Route de Targa, a good 20-min walk or a short taxi hop from the centre of Guéliz. The best public library in Marrakech with a good collection of books on Morocco and North Africa in French. Popular with local students.

Media

Main French- and English-language **newspapers** can be bought in pavement kiosks in Guéliz or major hotels. Morocco has an increasingly lively French language press. The weekly *Le Journal* provides acerbic comment and hard political news, while the weekly magazine *Tel Quel* is more analytical. For the official view, see *Le Matin du Sahara*. Political parties still have newspapers, including *Al Bayane*, *Libération*, and *L'Opinion*. The country's best-selling newspaper is the Arabic-language daily *Al Ahdath al maghribiya*. Morocco has two state-run **TV channels**, the stuffy *RTM*, broadcasting mainly in Arabic, and the livelier, former private channel, *2M*, www.2m.tv. Satellite television is also popular, with

Arabic and French news channels being particularly big. Morocco's most popular **radio** is the Tangiers-based *Médi-1*. Has local and international news in French and Arabic, mainstream western pop and Arabic music. Good special features occasionally.

Opticians
Wrede, 142 Av Mohammed V, Guéliz, **T** 044-435739. Professional optician, has products for contact lenses.

Pharmacies (late night)
Moroccan cities always have a *pharmacie de garde*, open at night or on public holidays. Other pharmacies will display the night/holiday duty rota on their doors. On Jemaâ el Fna, there is a small night pharmacy (*dépôt de nuit*) on the west side of the square. Closed Wed. Expect queues. The duty pharmacy in Guéliz will probably be better stocked. The main night pharmacy, on Rue Khalid ibn Oualid (street linking Bab Doukkala to post office square on Av Mohammed V), **T** 044-430415.

Police
The *Sûreté nationale*, **T** 19 (white vans with red/green stripe), are urban police. The *Gendarmerie royale* (grey uniforms) deal with rural areas, and wait on motor-cycles on country roads to catch speeders. Marrakech also has a tourist police, the *Brigade touristique*, set up to reduce the hassle to which visitors were once subject.

Post offices
The main PO in Marrakech, a big modernist concrete structure, is on Place du 16 Novembre/Av Mohammed V, Guéliz. *Open 0830-1215 and 1430-1845, Mon-Thu, Fri and Sat 0830-1130.* Poste restante service for long-stay travellers. In the médina, there's the main PO right on Jemaâ el Fna. Western Union service available, get there early as queues are long. Stamps are sometimes available from newsagents and tabacs. Letters to France and Spain, 6dh, rest

of Europe, 6dh 50. Letter boxes, not very common, are yellow.
Parcel post to Europe is expensive, 1kg will set you back 150dh.

Public holidays

See p172 for dates of Muslim holidays. Secular public holidays are
as follows: New Year's Day (1 January); 11 Jan (Manifesto for
Independence); 1 May (International Labour Day); 30 Jul (Fête du
Trône, commemorating present king's accession); 14 Aug
(Commemoration of the allegiance of Saharan provinces); 20 Aug
(Anniversary of the Revolution of King and People); 21 Aug (Youth
Day or Fête de la Jeunesse); 6 Nov (Anniversary of the Green
March, El Massira el Khadra, to reclaim Morocco's Spanish-
occupied southern provinces); 18 Nov (Independence in 1956 and
Mohammed V's return from exile).

Religious services

For information on Catholic church services at the **Eglise des
Saints-Martyrs**, Rue Imam Ali, Guéliz, **T** 044-430585. **Protestant
church**, 89 Blvd Moulay Rachid, **T** 044-431479.

Student organizations

Université Cadi Ayyad, Daoudiyat, a new neighbourhood north
of the médina, which has large law and arts faculties, is undergoing
a fair amount of turmoil. Rigourist Muslim and left-leaning student
groups regularly clash, without things ever spilling out into the
world beyond the campus.

Taxi firms

There are no private taxi firms as such. Drivers work for themselves
on the whole as taxi licences are given to individuals. See p29.

Telephone

There are coin-phones outside the main post office on Av
Mohammed V, Guéliz. The best place to make a call from is one of

the numerous telephone shops or téléboutiques. Some phones only take the older, 'silver-all-over' 5dh coins. If phoning abroad, get plenty of 5dh pieces from the man at the change desk. Not all téléboutiques allow reverse-charge calls (*un appel en PCV*). If you are in Morocco for any length of time, it may be worth getting a local chip to put in your mobile. There are two service providers, Maroc-Télécom, also known as IAM (for Ittisalat al Maghrib), and Méditel. The former has the better national coverage, the latter is slightly cheaper. Calls still work out expensive for locals and a lot of Moroccans just have phones to text message or beep each other. See also p26.

Time
Time is one hour behind GMT in winter, two hours in summer, ie in summer, if it's 2000 in Morocco, it'll be 2200 in the UK. Make sure you check carefully in spring and autumn to avoid missing a return flight.

Toilets
Staying in cheaper accommodation you'll come across a lot of yeti-foot Turkish loos. Cafés in modern areas will generally have sit-down rather than squat equipment for customer use. Cheap barbecue restaurants will not generally have loos. In old neighbourhoods, many homes do not have bathrooms, and people may go to the mosque's ablutions facility or *mirhadh* to wash and use the toilet (separate entrance). If taken short in the médina, this is one option. Ask for *la toilette* or the *el kabina*.

Transport enquiries
Aéroport de la Menara, **T** 044-368520. **ONCF** (trains), **T** 044-446569, www.oncf.ma. **Bab Doukkala Gare Routière** (buses), **T** 044-433933 (don't expect too much of this). **CTM** (private bus lines), Casablanca central info-line, **T** 022-458824, Marrakech information **T** 044-448328, www.ctm.co.ma. Best to turn up at

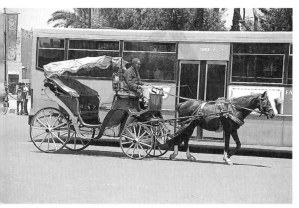

Marrakech transport
Orange buses to match the ochre city; ageing calèches to take a spin along the rampart roads.

their office next to Cinéma Colisée, Guéliz, day before you wish to travel. **Royal Air Maroc** (airline), **T** 044-425500/01. **Supratours** (private bus-line RAK to Essaouira), **T** 044-776520. There is no central information service for grand taxi services. These run between main towns from taxi ranks generally located near the bus stations. First departures are early morning, last departures between 1700 and 1900, depending on the time of year.

Travel agents
Most of the main reliable agencies have offices in Guéliz. **Adrar Aventure**, 111 Cité Saâda, Menara, **T** 044-435663, www.adrar-aventure.com. Agency set up by a qualified mountain guide from Imlil. Good range of mountain treks. **Atlas-Sahara Trek**, 6 bis Rue Houdhoud, Quartier Majorelle, **T** 044-313901. One of the best trekking agencies in Marrakech with 18 years' experience. Moroccan-born founder Bernard Fabry knows his deserts well. Also

runs upmarket accommodation in the Vallée des Aït Bougmez. **Erg Tours**, 22 Av Mohammed V, **T** 044-438471. Landrover hire. **High Country**, 31 Bab Amadil, Amizmiz, **T** 044-454847 (manager Matthew Low). Agency based in Amizmiz in the foothills of the High Atlas. Organizes rock climbing, off-roading, mountaineering, canoeing. Recommended. **Mohammed Nour**, **T/F** 044-302189. Organises treks in the High Atlas. English-speaking. **TTM-Trekking Tour Maroc**, 107 Rue Saâd Ben Errabia, Issil, **T** 044-308055. Offers ski trekking in Toubkal from 15 Jan-30 Apr, camel trekking by the Atlantic coast, mountain walking guides, meals and all camping equipment provided. **Pampa Voyage (Maroc)**, Imm. Jassim, 219 Blvd Mohammed V, Guéliz, **T** 044-431052, www.pampamaroc.com. Another agency with a good reputation. See also p32.

A sprint through history

703 AD	Mouassa ibn Noussayr conquers the western Maghreb, beginning the conversion of the Imazighen to Islam. Tangiers falls in 704.
1055	Under the banner of Islam, Almoravid tribal warriors move northwards from the Sahara into what is now Morocco. They first settle at Aghmat, near the mouth of the Ourika Valley.
1071	Foundation of Marrakech by Youssef ben Tachfine, first ruler of the Almoravid dynasty. Beginnings of the palm groves.
1106-43	Reign of the Almoravid sultan Ali ben Youssef. Construction of the ramparts and the first *khettaras* (underground 'canals') to supply the city with water.
1147	Marrakech falls to Almohads, bearers of a new, rigourist brand of Islam.
1199	Death of Almohad sultan Abd el Moumen. Completion of the Koutoubia Mosque.
1269	Marrakech falls to the Merinids and loses its status of capital to Fès.
1465	Collapse of the Merinids as the Portuguese make inroads on the coast.
1492	Granada falls to the Catholic monarchs, Ferdinand and Isabella. End of Islamic rule in Andalusia. Skilled refugees flee to North Africa.
1578	Sultan Mansour Eddhabi, 'the Golden', triumphs over the Portuguese at the Battle of the Three Kings near Larache.

1594	Construction of the Badi or 'Wondrous' Palace by Mansour Eddhabi. Marrakech once more capital.
1707	Destruction of the Badi Palace by sultan Moulay Ismaïl. Power is now centred on the new imperial capital of Meknès.
1764	Sultan Mohammed ben Abdallah decides to create a new port on the Atlantic, west of Marrakech. Essaouira is built and is an important port by 1780.
1828	Replantation of the Agdal gardens.
1894	Death of Hassan I. Ba Ahmed becomes Grand Vizier. Construction of the Bahia Palace.
1912	Morocco is divided into French and Spanish protectorates. French forces under Colonel Mangin enter Marrakech. Under the influence of Résident-Général Maréchal Lyautey, the city acquires the new garden suburb of Guéliz. Ascendancy of the Glaoui family in the south, following the development of mines by French companies which ensure the family's wealth.
1925	Revolt in the Rif (northwest Morocco), French and Spanish rule threatened. Lyautey dismissed. Maréchal Pétain puts down revolt with great brutality – aeroplanes used to bomb civilian populations for first time.
1929	The palm groves of Marrakech are declared a protected zone.
1930	Population of Marrakech reaches 60,000.
1956	Moroccan independence from France.
1960	City population reaches 243,000.

1961	Death of Mohammed V. Accession of his son as Hassan II.
1971, 72	Two attempted *coups d'état* nearly overthrow the Alaouite dynasty.
1975	Al Massira el Khadra, the Green March. Monarchy reinforces its authority with a peaceful march by over 100,000 Moroccans to reclaim Spanish-held Saharan territories on the Atlantic coast. Régime's legitimacy reinforced.
1975-91	'*Les années de plomb*', 'the leaden years', period of severe repression for all forms of political opposition to the régime.
1981	Rioting in Morocco's major cities, Marrakech included, is put down with great violence.
1982	Population of Marrakech reaches 440,000.
1992	Publication in France of Gilles Perrault's *Notre ami le roi*, a severe critique of Hassan II's rule. Paradoxically, the régime begins to loosen its hold on civil society.
1996	French TV channel M6's programme *Capital* screens a documentary on French 'bourgeois-bohemians' restoring houses in the old neighbourhoods of Marrakech for 'a handful of francs'. Gentrification of the médina is under way. Housing for low income groups in the new Massira I, II and III housing areas on the Essaouira road.
1999	July: death of Hassan II. Accession of his eldest son as Mohammed VI. November: Driss Basri, oppressive minister of the interior, is sacked. Climate of growing political freedom.

2000	Population of the Greater Marrakech area reaches 1,000,000. The Circuit de la Palmeraie continues to grow as an upmarket residential zone.
2001	October: unfortunate events in the USA notwithstanding, the first session of the Marrakech International Film Festival is a huge success. Plans for a new hotel zone, near the airport, are launched.
2002	General elections. The PJD, a 'Muslim-Democrat' party, emerges as the main opposition party.
2003	May: Morocco shaken by terrorist suicide bombings by Islamic rigourists in Casablanca. October: a major reform of the *Moudawana*, the personal status code, is announced by the King. The reform looks set to make a huge improvement in women's conditions.
2006	Completion of the autoroute link to Casablanca?

Art and architecture

Origins of Moroccan cities

In 682, an Arab army swept into the Maghreb from the Near East, bearer of the revealed religion of Islam. As cities were founded, new building types appeared, shaped by the requirements of prayer and Muslim life. The mosque evolved from its humble beginnings as open holy precinct to become a spectacular edifice demonstrating the power of dynasties. The emblem of Marrakech, the Koutoubia Mosque, is just such a building.

Mosques

In all Muslim countries, mosques are built orientated towards Mecca, as the believers must pray facing their holy city. In Morocco this means that the orientation is east-south-east. A large mosque will have prayer halls, courtyard and colonnades, minaret, and, in all likelihood, an ablutions facility and hammam. The first minarets were probably developed in the late seventh century, put up by Christian builders copying the square towers of Syrian churches. Moroccan minarets are generally a simple square tower with a small 'lantern' feature on the top, from which the *muezzin* makes the call to prayer. Older minarets feature blind horseshoe arches and a small dome on the topmost 'lantern' room. Islam does not favour figurative representation, so instead of sculpture elaborate geometric forms in ceramic mosaic (*zellige*), or carved on wood and plaster decorate ceilings and walls.

Medersas

The non-Muslim visitor can observe Muslim sacred architecture by visiting the Medersa Ben Youssef in

Marrakech, a major college in the Moroccan education system from medieval times onward. Rebuilt in the 16th century, it has all the main decorative features: a courtyard with reflecting pool, ceramic mosaic, and densely carved stucco and cedar wood. The austere students' rooms come as something of a shock after the elaborate decoration of the courtyard.

Médina

The Koutoubia excepted, city mosques and medersas are generally packed in amongst the surrounding buildings. The confusing tangle of streets notwithstanding, the médina or old town has its specific logic, providing protection from both fierce summer sun and potential invaders. To maximize shade and space within the walls, streets were kept narrow. Although harbouring exotically-clothed populations, early European visitors saw the médina as chaotic and backward – the home of disease and ignorance. Today, however, the médina of Marrakech is home to numerous European gentrifiers.

Riads

The courtyard house, which goes back to classical antiquity, was adopted for family life across North Africa. It provides a high level of family privacy, important in Islam. In densely built-up cities, the roof terraces also provided a place for women to go about household tasks – and to share news and gossip. In Marrakech, the biggest houses or *riads* have several patios, the main one with impressive arcades on two levels. Extended families could thus be accommodated in dwellings with big open areas. Given the large numbers of houses now used as museums, restaurants and guesthouses,

Moroccan courtyard homes are easily visited today – see for example the late 19th-century Dar Marjana near Dar el Bacha or the Maison Tiskiwine.

High Atlas villages

Walkers may spend nights in homes in the Atlas. At strategic points in the mountain valleys, the villages of the Imazighen form compact masses of building. Houses are virtually wedged onto the hillside, slotting into each other, taking advantage of every bump and dip of the terrain. Built entirely with local materials, these *douar* merge perfectly with the reds, browns and greys of the landscape. With community interests predominant, individual houses are a rarity.

20th-century Marrakech

The structure of contemporary Marrakech is very much an early 20th-century achievement, the work the first French Resident-Général Maréchal Lyautey and urban planner Henri Prost. Between 1912 and 1928, the tree-lined streets of the modern centre, Guéliz, and the Hivernage garden suburb were laid out. A grand new avenue focusing on the Koutoubia linked old and new neighbourhoods while the médina's ramparts were preserved as a buffer zone. New construction, characterized by simple forms and functionality, took on the contours of traditional building. Craft techniques were used for detailing, giving a 'Moroccan style' to otherwise modern buildings. Historic monuments were conserved and a decree turned the centuries-old Palmeraie, into a protected zone, a situation which lasted into the 1980s. In recent years, there has been a huge renewal of interest in Marrakech's historic architecture, notably packed-earth construction in the médina.

Books

Fiction

Binebine, M, *Pollens*. (2002), Casablanca: Le Fennec, Paris: Julliard. If you read French, anything by Binebine is a must. *Pollens* is the tale of a young French couple who through *kif* are trapped in a remote village. Earlier novels include *Les funérailles du lait*, *Le sommeil de l'esclave*, *L'ombre du poète* and *Cannibales*.

Freud, E, *Hideous Kinky*. (1992), Penguin. A child's view of travels with a hippy mother in search of primal religious experience. Some good sequences as mum strives to understand sufi Islam while kids muck in with the street urchins of Jemaâ el Fna. Hilarious and pathetic. (See also late 1990s film starring Saïd Tangeaoui.)

Goytisolo, J, *Makbara*. (1993), Serpent's Tail. A surreal tale shifting between genders and cities, between Morocco, Paris and imagined otherwheres. A good companion on any travels.

Goytisolo, J, *The Garden of Secrets*. (2000), Serpent's Tail. A Decameron-like gathering recount the multiple lives of a mysterious writer settled in Marrakech. Reading for siesta time.

Non-fiction

Canetti, E, *The Voices of Marrakech*. (1954, 1967 translation), Marion Boyars. A classic. A few days were enough for Canetti to encapsulate the mysteries of Marrakech in 14 telling tableaux.

El Faiz, M, *Les Jardins de Marrakech*. (2000), Actes Sud. A historical introduction to the gardens and palm groves so essential to the city's atmosphere.

Guinaudeau, Z, *Traditional Moroccan Cooking*. (1994), Serif. Avoiding the lavish titles about someone's pricey and poncey restaurant, have a read of Mme Guinaudeau's thorough overview of Moroccan cooking. Unlikely ingredients and long preparation times are the key to many of the recipes.

Lamazou, K and T, *Sous les toits de terre*. (1988), Casablanca: Belvisi. Line and watercolour illustrations portraying a year in the life of Imelghas, a remote village up in the Vallée des Aït Bougmez, before electricity and the trekkers arrived. A must for those whose souvenir photographs failed to live up to expectations.

Marzouki, A, *Tazmamart, cellule 10*. (2000), Casablanca: Editions Tarak, Paris: Gallimard. A landmark in recent Moroccan publishing, an account by a former detainee of 18 years' imprisonment in inhuman conditions in the Moroccan outback. Of 58 officers, soldiers and pilots accused of participating in the failed coups of 1971 and 1972, and imprisoned at Tazmamart, only 28 survived. Further accounts by political prisoners in the *bagnes* (prisons) of Agdz, Kénitra and Kelaâ des Mgouna have followed.

Maxwell, G, *Lords of the Atlas*. (1966, 1983), Century Publishing. Classic portrait of the rise and fall of the Glaoui dynasty who ruled the Moroccan South from the Red City during the first half of the 20th century. With the end of French rule in 1956 came the family's disgrace. Maxwell was writing at a time when the splendours and autocratic cruelties of T'hami, Pacha of Marrakech, were still very much part of the city's memory.

Perrault, G, *Notre ami le Roi*. (1992), Paris: Gallimard. An uncompromising portrait of the first 30 years of Hassan II's reign by a journalist writing for local intellectuals. Though banned, the book was widely faxed over to Morocco and contributed substantially to a loosening of authoritarian rule.

Pochy, Y and **Triki**, H *Medersa de Marrakech*. (1990), Paris: EPA. Superb photographic portrait of the Red City's most venerable building, a lavish Muslim college which continued to function as a place of education within living memory.

Rogerson, B, editor *Marrakech, the Red City* (2003) London: Sickle Moon Books. Fogeyish anthology of writings on Marrakech. Insight from explorers and envoys, more recent material by Sacheverell Sitwell, George Orwell and Gavin Maxwell.

Ruthven, M, *Islam in the World*. (1984, 2000), Penguin. Possibly the best introduction to Islam. Not the lightest of reads, but filled with useful explanations and insight.

Language

For the English speaker, some of the sounds of Moroccan Arabic are totally alien. There is a strong glottal stop (as in the word 'bottle' when pronounced in Cockney English), generally represented by an apostrophe, and a rasping sound written here as 'kh', rather like the 'ch' of the Scots 'loch' or the Greek 'drachma'. And there is a glottal 'k' sound, which luckily often gets pronounced as the English hard 'g', and a very strongly aspirated 'h' (denoted in the list below by an upper case 'H') in addition to the weak 'h'. The French 'r' sound is generally transcribed as 'gh'. Anyway, don't worry: Moroccan acquaintances will have a fun time correcting your attempts at Arabic pronunciation.

Note that language politics in Morocco are complicated – the written form of **Arabic** is as remote from everyday spoken Arabic (*darija maghrebiya*) as medieval Latin is from Italian. **Tachelhit**, an Amazigh language is the main (unwritten) language of the mountains. Just to complicate the picture, Marrakech has an **Arabic dialect** of its own. Other Moroccans have to concentrate hard to understand it properly. Morocco's élite are generally strong in **French**, the country's second written language, and those who deal with tourists will have more than just a smattering of English. As French is so widespread, using French numbers and basic phrases is often enough to get some form of communication going. When dealing with people who've been deprived of schooling, the communication problem is not so much one of language as one of different mind-sets in understanding other's needs. Note that the illiteracy rate for women is estimated at 65%.

The following is a list of transliterated standard Arabic phrases. (A capital H is used to indicate the strongly aspirated H used by Moroccans; 'q' indicates the clicking 'k' sound).

Greetings, courtesies
Thank you *shukran*
Hi/goodbye *esslama; selam alaykum* (more formal)
Good day (until after lunch/mid-afternoon) *sebah el-khir*
Have a good evening *umsia sa'ida*
Goodnight *tesbeh ala khir*
Goodbye *bisslama*
please *'afek, men fedhlek*
I'm sorry, sir/madam *smeh-li assidi, elilla*
Excuse me *bellati, ils smehti*
It's my fault *el-felta diyali*
yes *eyyer, na'am, wakha*
no *la* (the 'a' is lengthened)
It's my pleasure *be-la jamil*

Buying and bargaining
shop *hanout*
money *leflous*
change *es-sarf*
How much is it? *Be-chHal et-temene?*
It's a good product *Hadi sela'a sHiHa*
But it's expensive/cheap *We-lekin ghaliya/rkhissa*

It's a good price *Et-temen mezyen*
Add some more! *Zid-ni chi-hajja!*
I'm not going to give you more *Ma nzid-k hatta frank*
By God, you're a tough bargainer! *Nari, ch-Hal sa'ib!*
Do you have change? *'Indek es-sarf?*

Getting around

Where's the bus station? *fayn kayna mahattet el-kirene?*
bridge *qantra*
straight ahead *níshan*
to the right/left *ila l-yemin / sh-shimal*
turn at the corner *dour fil-qent*
ticket *bitaqa*, also *warqa* (lit 'paper')
train *qitar*
How much is the ticket? *Aysh Hal taman diyal warqa?*
Speak slowly please! *Tekellem bishweyya min fedlek!*
Could you write that down please? *'Afak, uktebhu liya?*

Accommodation

room *el-bít*
bed *tliq, farsh*
mattress *talmíta*
shower *douche*
without shower *bila douche*
key *es sarrout*
blanket *ghta'*
sheet *izar*
noise *sda'*
At the hotel – a few requests and complaints
Can I see the room, please? *Afak, mumkin nshouf el bít?*
The water's off *El ma maktou'a*
There's no hot water *El-ma skhoun ma ka'insh*
Excuse me, are there any towels? *Afak ka'in foutet?*
Could you bring us some towels? *Mumkin tjíbilna foutet?*

The washbasin's blocked   *El lavabo makhnouk*
The window doesn't close   *Esh sherajim ma yetsidoush*
The toilet flush doesn't work   *La chasse ma tekhdemsh*
There's a lot of noise   *Ka'in sda' bezef*
Can I change rooms?   *Mumkin nebedil el bít?*

At the café
tea with mint   *ettay be-na'na'*
coffee   *qahwa*
strong milky coffee   *qahwa mherssa*
bottle of water   *gara diyel ma*
still water   *Sidi Ali, Sidi Harazem* (brands)
fizzy water   *Oulmès, Bonacqua* (brands)
small/large bottle   *gara sghira/kbira*
orange juice   *asir limoun*

Question words
How?   *kif-aysh?*
When?   *fawq-aysh?*
Where?   *fayne?*
Why?   *alaysh?*
What's this?   *eshnou hada?*

Useful phrases
Where are the loos?   *Fayne kayn la kabina, les toilettes?*
I didn't understand   *Ma fhemt-shi mezyen*
Enough, enough, enough!   *Safi, baraka, saline!*
Calm down, be reasonable! (Polite)   *Ellah yehdik!*
That's a shameful (thing to say/do).   *'Ib aleek*
Leave me alone, please!   *Khelli-ni trankil, afek!*

Numbers
zero *sifr*, 1 *wahid*, 2 *itnine*, 3 *tleta*, 4 *erb'a*, 5 *khamsa*, 6 *setta*, 7 *seb'a*, 8 *tmeniya*, 9 *tess'oud*, 10 *'ashra*, 11 *eHdash*, 12 *itnash*,

13 *tletash,* 14 *rbe'ttashi,* 15 *khmestash,* 16 *settash,* 17 *sbe'tash,*
18 *tmentash,* 19 *ti'ssatash,* 20 *ishrine,* 21 *wahid-we-ishrine,*
22 *itnine-we-ishrine,* 30 *tletine,* 40 *arba'ine,* 50 *khamsine,*
60 *sittine,* 70 *sba'ine,* 80 *tmenine,* 90 *tiss'ine,* 100 *miya,*
200 *miatayn,* 1000 *alf.*

Glossary

In the city

bab   gate

bildi   'of the countryside', ie anything authentic, traditional

borj   tower

derb   street, and by extension, neighbourhood

hammam   traditional Moroccan public bath

idhan   call to prayer made by the *muezzin*

fantasia   traditional cavalry charges, originally held during
  banquets in honour of the governor or king

fondouk   merchants' hostel

gaouri   foreign, sometimes derogatory

kissariya   informal shopping arcade

makhzen   term used to designate the Moroccan state, centring on
  the palace

mechouar   open area near palace, used for ceremonies

medersa   school

mellah   former Jewish area of a city

moucharabiya   latticework window grill

kasbah   fortress

nasrani   lit 'from Nazareth', and therefore, foreign

qibla   niche in interior wall of a mosque indicating direction
  of Mecca

koubba   dome

pisé   adobe, packed earth.

riad   courtyard city residence, many now used as guesthouses *roumi*   modern, opposite of *bildi*

souk   covered market

skala   seaside ramparts of a port

tadelakt   hard plaster rendering, typical of the hammams of Marrakech, now popular for decoration

zaouia   shrine to an Islamic holy person

zelliges   ceramic mosaic work, much used on interior walls.

In the country

amazigh pl *imazighen*   Berber

douar   village

kasbah   fortress

moussem   annual country festival, originally held in honour of a holy person

trig   road

About food

bastila   speciality of Fès, filo pastry stuffed with pigeon, almonds, egg, sprinkled with sugar and cinnamon

kefta   minced meat

etriya   spices

khli'   salt, dried meat

lHem begri   beef

lHem ghenmi   mutton

mechoui   barbecued meat

qetbene   brochettes

mfewwer   steamed

m'Hemmer   roasted

tajine   meat and vegetables slow cooked in an earthenware pot or *tajine*

tanjia   lamb in a terracotta jar slow cooked in the embers of a hammam oven

Index

Credits

Footprint credits
Editor: Sarah Thorowgood
Map editor: Sarah Sorensen

Publisher: Patrick Dawson
Series created by: Rachel Fielding
In-house cartography: Claire Benison,
Kevin Feeney, Robert Lunn.
Proofreading: Stephanie Egerton

Design: Mytton Williams
Maps: Footprint Handbooks Ltd

Photography credits
Front cover: Jeremy Horner/Panos
Pictures, handmade slippers
Inside: Patrick Syder, Claire Boobbyer
Cut out images: p1 Koutoubia Mosque,
p5 lamp from médina souk, p35
Almoravid Koubba, p63 camel at
Essaouira
Generic images: John Matchett
Back cover: Claire Boobbyer

Print
Manufactured in Italy by LegoPrint

Footprint feedback
We try as hard as we can to make
each Footprint guide as up to date
as possible but, of course, things
always change. If you want to let us
know about your experiences – good,
bad or ugly – then don't delay, go
www.footprintbooks.com and send
in your comments.
® Footprint Handbooks and the Footprint
mark are a registered trademark of
Footprint Handbooks Ltd

Publishing information
Footprint 2004
1st edition
Text and maps © Footprint Handbooks
Ltd May 2004

ISBN 1 903471 81 8
CIP DATA: a catalogue record for this
book is available from the British Library

Published by Footprint
6 Riverside Court
Lower Bristol Road
Bath BA2 3DZ, UK
T+44 (0)1225 469141
F+44 (0)1225 469461
discover@footprintbooks.com
www.footprintbooks.com

Distributed in the USA by Publishers
Group West

Complete title list

Latin America & Caribbean

Argentina
Barbados (P)
Bolivia
Brazil
Caribbean Islands
Central America & Mexico
Chile
Colombia
Costa Rica
Cuba
Cusco & the Inca Trail
Dominican Republic
Ecuador & Galápagos
Guatemala
Havana (P)
Mexico
Nicaragua
Peru
Rio de Janeiro
South American Handbook
Venezuela

North America

New York (P)
Vancouver (P)
Western Canada

Africa

Cape Town (P)
East Africa
Libya
Marrakech &
  the High Atlas
Morocco
Namibia
South Africa
Tunisia
Uganda

Middle East

Egypt
Israel
Jordan
Syria & Lebanon

Asia

Bali
Bangkok & the Beaches
Cambodia
Goa
Hong Kong (P)
India
Indian Himalaya
Indonesia
Laos
Malaysia
Myanmar (Burma)
Nepal
Pakistan
Rajasthan & Gujarat
Singapore
South India
Sri Lanka
Sumatra
Thailand
Tibet
Vietnam

Australasia

Australia
East Coast Australia
New Zealand
Sydney (P)
West Coast Australia

Europe

Andalucía
Barcelona
Barcelona (P)
Berlin (P)
Bilbao (P)
Bologna (P)
Britain
Cardiff (P)
Copenhagen (P)
Croatia
Dublin (P)
Edinburgh (P)
England
Glasgow
Glasgow (P)
Ireland
Lisbon (P)
London
London (P)
Madrid (P)
Naples (P)
Northern Spain
Paris (P)
Reykjavik (P)
Scotland
Scotland Highlands
  & Islands
Seville (P)
Spain
Tallinn (P)
Turin (P)
Turkey
Valencia (P)
Verona (P)

(P) denotes pocket
Handbook

Publishing stuff

Publishing stuff

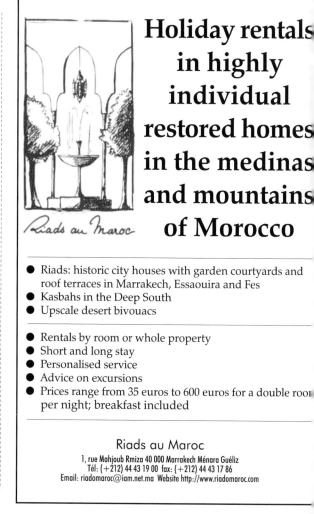

RIAD ZINOUN

Michelle and Said welcome you with a decor that will remind you of a tale of the one thousand and one nights. After spending the day at the colourful souks and a walk to the famous *Jamaa el fna* plaza 180m from the riad, you will be able to rest and enjoy the sun on a quiet terrace with its beautiful view of the mountains covered with snow, drinking a fresh fruit juice cocktail. You can then sample the fabulous Moroccan cuisine on the patio.

We also organise performances of traditional berber songs and Andalousian music as well as the transing music of the Gnawa.

Rates start at €50 including breakfast in the low season. For our latest rate see www.riadzinoun.com.

"Votre bien être est notre rasion d'être"
Your feeling good is our only concern.

Riad Zinoun
31, Derb Ben Amrane
Riad Zitoun Kedim
4000 Marrakech
T/F 00 212 44 42 67 93
www.riadzinoun.com

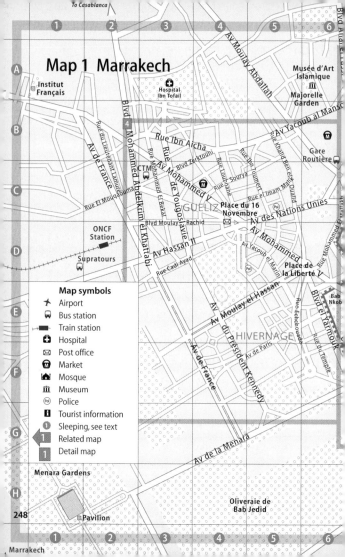

Map 1 Marrakech

To Casablanca

Institut
Français

Hospital
Ibn Tofail

Musée d'Art
Islamique

Majorelle
Garden

Av Moulay Abdallah

Av Yacoub al Mansour

Rue du Lieutenant Lamure

Rue Ibn Aicha

Rue Ibn Zaid

Blvd Zerktouni

Rue el Khatib Ben el Ouadid

Gare
Routière

Av de France

Blvd Mohammed Abdelkrim el Khattabi

Rue Mohammed El Béqal

Rue Mohammed El Béqal

Rue Loubnane

Rue Sourya

Rue el Imam Malik

CTM

Av de Yougoslavie

GUELIZ

Place du 16
Novembre

Av des Nations Unies

Rue El Mouqaouma

Blvd Moulay Rachid

Av Mohammed

Rue Mohammed el Ma…

ONCF
Station

Av Hassan II

Av Yacoub el Mansour

Place de
la Liberté

Supratours

Rue Cadi Ayad

Bab
Nkob

Map symbols

✈ Airport
🚌 Bus station
🚂 Train station
✚ Hospital
✉ Post office
🏪 Market
🕌 Mosque
🏛 Museum
Ⓟ Police
ℹ Tourist information
➊ Sleeping, see text
◀➊ Related map
➊ Detail map

HIVERNAGE

Av Moulay el Hassan

Rue Échouhada

Rue du Temple

Blvd el Yarmouk

Av du Président Kennedy

Av de Paris

Av de France

Menara Gardens

248

Av de la Menara

Oliveraie de
Bab Jedid

Pavilion

Marrakech

To Casablanca

Blvd Allal el Fassi

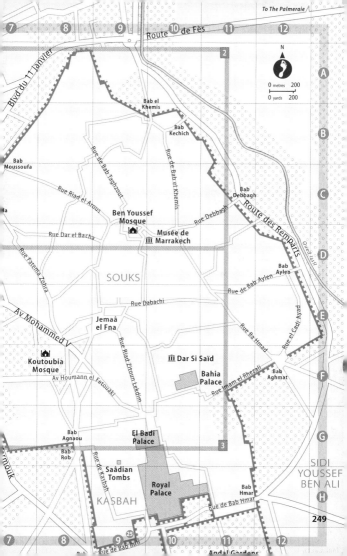

To The Palmeraie

Route de Fès

2

N

0 metres 200
0 yards 200

A

Blvd du 11 Janvier

Bab el Khemis

Bab Kechich

Bab Moussoufa

B

Rue de Bab Taghzout

Rue de Bab el Khemis

Bab Debbagh

C

Rue Riad el Arous

Rue Debbagh

Route des Remparts

Ben Youssef Mosque

Oued Issil

Musée de Marrakech

D

Rue Dar el Bacha

Bab Aylen

SOUKS

Rue de Bab Aylen

Rue Fatema Zohra

Rue Dabachi

E

Rue Ba Hmad

Rue el Gadr Ayad

Av Mohammed V

Jemaâ el Fna

Rue Riad Zitoun Lekdim

Dar Si Saïd

Koutoubia Mosque

Bahia Palace

Bab Aghmat

F

Av Houmann el Fetouaki

Rue Imam el Rhezali

Bab Agnaou

El Badi Palace

G

3

Bab-Rob

-mouk

Saâdian Tombs

SIDI YOUSSEF BEN ALI

Rue de Kasbah

Royal Palace

Bab Hmar

H

KASBAH

Rue de Bab Hmar

249

Rue de Bab Itrh

25

Agdal Gardens

N

| 0 metres | 100 |
| 0 yards | 100 |

A

SOUK
EL KHEMIS

B

AA
ECHRA

Route des Remparts

C

Rue el Mechra

Oued Issil

Rue de Sidi Ghalem

Bab el
Khemis

D

ZAOUIA
SIDI GHALEM

Bab
Khechich

1

Rue de Bab Taghzoult

Rue Assouel

BAB EL
KHEMIS

E

KECHICH

Rue de Bab El Khemis

F

AS SOUEL

RIAD
ROUSSE

G

EL MOUKEF

ZAOUIA
LAHDAR

HART
ES SOURA

Tanneries

H

Ben
Youssef
Mosque

Dar
Bellarj

Medersa
Ben Youssef

Bab
Debbagh
251

Place Ben Youssef

Rue Souk Ahl Fass

Rue Debbagh

Tanneries

Almoravid
Koubba

Rue Es

DAR DEBBAGH

Hammam   Musée de

Map 3 Jemaâ el Fna & around

MZOUGA

R'MILA

MOUAS

Av Ahmed Ouakha

Bab Er Raha

Town Hall

Rue El Adala

Hammam du Pacha

Rue Fatema Zahra

Rue Sidi el Yamani

Ensemble Artesanal

Piscine de la Koutoubia

Rue Abou el Abbes

Av Mohammed V

LEKSOUR

Trek el Koutoubia

Bab Sidi Ghrib

Square Foucauld

Koutoubia Mosque

ARSET EL BILK

Rue Moulay Ismail

Koutoubia Rose Garden

Rue Ben Marine

Bab Jedid

Av Houman el Ferouaki

RIAD ZIT EL KED

Blvd el Yarmouk

Rue Lalla Fikia

Rue Ibn Rachid

Rue Okba Ben Nafia

Rue Sidi Mimoune

ARSE MA

SIDI MIMOUN

BAB AGNAOU

N

0 metres 100
0 yards 100

Bab Agnaou

Kasbah Mosque

Bab Rob

252

LAHDAR ES SOURA

Tanneries

Bab Debbagh

⑦

Ben Youssef Mosque ⑧

Dar Bellarj

⑨ ②

⑩ ⑪

⑫

Tanneries

Medersa Ben Youssef

Almoravid Koubba

Place Ben Youssef

Rue Souk Ahl Fass

DAR DEBBAC

Hammam Ben Youssef

Musée de Marrakech

ESSEBTIYNE

Ⓐ

Kissarias

KAÂT BENHADID

SOUKS

ouassine Mosque

Criée Berbère

Rahba Kedima

AZBEZT

Ⓑ

RAHBA KEDIMA ④

③

BEN SALAH

ARSET SIDI YOUSSEF

Souk Larzal

⑧

Rue de Bab Aylen

Ⓒ

ARSET MOULAY BOUAZZA

⑥

Rue Debbachi

DERB DEBBACHI ⑤

Rue Sidi Boulabada

KENNARIA

Derb Jedid

ARSET EL HOUTA

Ⓓ

①

⑨

mam Zitoun edim ㉘

㉖

㉙

DOUAR GRAOUA

Ⓔ

Dar Si Saïd

JNANE BEN CHEGRA

Ⓕ

Maison Tiskiwine

EL JEDID

㉗

Bahia Palace

Ⓖ

Rue Imam el Rhezali

Ⓗ

253

TOURARIA

Place des Ferblantiers

MELLAH

Bab Berrima

El Badi Palace

⑦

⑧

⑨ ①

⑩

⑪

⑫

BERRIMA

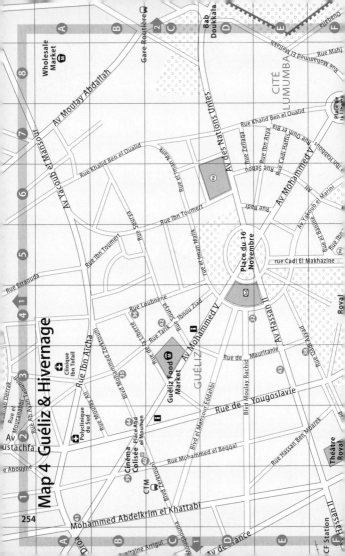

Bab Nkob

Blvd el Yarmouk

Rue el Khattab

Rue el Khafajah

Ornane

Rue Echchouada

Rue Ibn el Khattib

Rue el Khatib

Rue A El kahini

Rue Ahmed Chaouqi

Rue Hafid Ibrahim

Av du Temple

Av El Qadisia

Av de Paris

Rue el Matzouzi

Rue Ibrahim el Mazini

Bab Jedid

Rue Haroun Errachid

Av de la Menara

HIVERNAGE

Stadi al Harti

Av Moulay Hassan

Av du Président Kennedy

Av de Paris

Rue Ben Badis

Rue Nador

Rue Al Houstayma

Rue Ibn Oudari

Rue el Abdelmalek

Rue el Ksar el Kbir

Rue el Aradch

Rue Chechaouen

Av El Qadisia

Président Kennedy

Av de France

Palais des Congrès

Av de France

Rue Ibn Abdoun

Benna

Rue Bel Khatab

Rue Abou Bakr

Rue Ibn el Chat

255

N

0 metres 100
0 yards 100

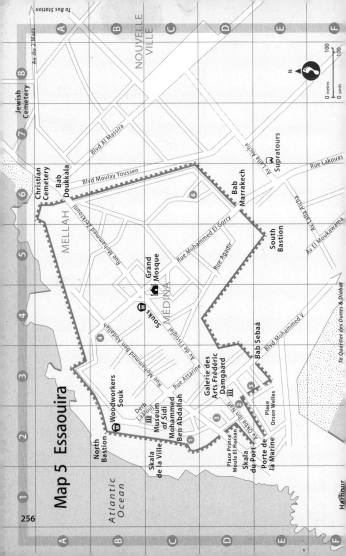

Map 5 Essaouira

256

Atlantic Ocean

To Bus Station

NOUVELLE VILLE

Av du 2 Mars

Jewish Cemetery

Christian Cemetery

Blvd Al Massira

Bab Doukkala

Blvd Moulay Youssen

MELLAH

Rue Mohammed Zerktouni

Grand Mosque

MÉDINA

Souks

Rue Mohammed El Gorry

Rue Agadir

Bab Marrakech

South Bastion

Av Lalla Aicha

Supratours

Rue Lakouas

Av Lalla Aicha

Av El Moukawama

Woodworkers Souk

North Bastion

Skala de la Ville

Derb Laalouj

Museum of Sidi Mohammed Ben Abdallah

Rue Mohammed Ben Abdallah

Av de l'Istiqlal

Rue Attarine

Galerie des Arts-Frédéric Damgaard

Bab Sebaâ

Blvd Mohammed V

Av Oqba Ibn Nafi

Place Prince Moula El Hassan

Skala du Port

Porte de la Marine

Place Orson Welles

Harbour

To Quartier des Dunes & Diabat

N

0 metres 100
0 yards 100